Advancing Social Justice

Advancing
Social Justice

Tools, Pedagogies, and Strategies
to Transform Your Campus

Tracy Davis
Laura M. Harrison

Foreword by Larry D. Roper

JB JOSSEY-BASS™
A Wiley Brand

Copyright © 2013 by John Wiley & Sons, Inc. All rights reserved.

Published by Jossey-Bass
A Wiley Brand
One Montgomery Street, Suite 1200, San Francisco, CA 94104-4594-www.josseybass.com

Consulting editor: John Schuh

Jossey-Bass books and products are available through most bookstores. To contact Jossey-Bass directly, call our Customer Care Department within the U.S. at 800-956-7739, outside the U.S. at 317-572-3986, or fax 317-572-4002.

Wiley publishes in a variety of print and electronic formats and by print-on-demand. Some material included with standard print versions of this book may not be included in e-books or in print-on-demand. If this book refers to media such as a CD or DVD that is not included in the version you purchased, you may download this material at http://book support.wiley.com. For more information about Wiley products, visit www.wiley.com.

Library of Congress Cataloging-in-Publication Data

Davis, Tracy

Advancing social justice: tools, pedagogies, and strategies to transform your campus / Tracy Davis, Laura M. Harrison. -- First edition.
        pages cm. -- (The Jossey-Bass higher and adult education series)
Includes bibliographical references and index.
ISBN 978-1-118-38843-3 (hardback); ISBN 978-1-118-41751-5 (ebk.);
ISBN 978-1-118-42208-3 (ebk.)
 1. Social justice--Study and teaching (Higher) 2. Education, Higher--Social aspects.
 3. Critical pedagogy. I. Harrison, Laura M. II. Title.
 LC192.2D4 2013
 370.11'5--dc23

                                                    2013013518

Printed in the United States of America
FIRST EDITION
HB Printing   10 9 8 7 6 5 4 3 2 1

The Jossey-Bass
Higher and Adult Education Series

Contents

List of Tables and Exhibits

Tables

Exhibits

From Tracy

I dedicate this book to Janet and DeWayne Davis, who nurtured in me a sense of justice, allowed me to fail, and taught me the fundamentals of equity and inclusion, and to Marjorie, Tyler, and Evan, who remind me to practice what I teach.

From Laura

I dedicate this book to Dan Harrison, who first taught me about justice, and Christy Zempter, who empowers me to become my most authentic self.

Foreword

The journey toward the focus on social justice in higher education has taken a winding and sometimes confusing path. During my more than thirty-five-year career, I have participated in conversations and educational activity focused on such topics as "managing diversity," "dealing with difference," "multiculturalism," "pluralism," and many other descriptors. While much of the effort to affect access, inclusion, and positive climate for diversity has been well intentioned, it has too often been poorly framed and lacking in conceptual rigor—the desired positive effects of our work have too often been undermined by the inadequacy of the frameworks to which our efforts have been attached.

The social justice movement brings with it a new promise. Social justice, when pursued according to its true meaning, provides a frame that compels educators to think and act in a more dedicated and compassionate way toward all students; professionals committed to social justice will advocate for treating all students in a humane and dignified manner. A focused approach to social justice has the potential to profoundly alter the texture of our relationships with learners and transform the landscape of the learning climate on our campuses. Even more, if we sincerely embrace what it means to be a social justice educator, our connection to the world and the dynamics of our relationships will reveal new levels of awareness, commitment, and accountability for the conditions that we create and the effects of our ways of being on all with whom we have interaction. If we take the social justice imperative seriously, we will move beyond advocacy and commit to transforming who we are in our relationships with others.

While acting in a socially just manner can be described in a simple and easy-to-comprehend way, true social justice is much more difficult to achieve. Our assessment of human nature tells us that most of us carry in our hearts a deep desire to be fair and just in our treatment of others—we want to be architects of inclusive and caring networks that advance the common good. At the same time, each of us carries within us our own political ideologies, spiritual or religious outlooks, conscious and unconscious socialization, and deeply held personal values (some of which we have not examined). We are too often not aware of the strength of our perspectives and how our beliefs about particular groups and issues influence the ways in which we communicate or affect our ability to create space for others in conversations or learning experiences.

The power of *Advancing Social Justice* is its direct challenge to us to take a step back from where we are, do an honest and unvarnished assessment of how we currently practice social justice, to rethink how we approach our work, and to recommit and reengage in accordance with a more informed and more rigorous conceptual framework. Tracy Davis and Laura M. Harrison remind us that social justice demands equitable distribution of resources, as well as commitment to methods that allow full participation by all: social justice is not just a matter of expressed values, but how we use our knowledge, skills, and power to construct educational practice to allow access and inclusion in the learning process. Social Justice 2.0, as coined by the authors, advances a depth of relationship between educators and learners that we have either avoided or failed to recognize.

Social Justice 2.0 has at its foundation deep respect and regard for the personhood of all students; in place of harsh judgment of the attitudes and perspectives presented by the learner, the educator will offer care and commitment to helping the student successfully navigate the path to deep and personally meaningful awareness. A new approach to social justice demands that we have affection for the learner, regardless of the degree to which the student's attitudes or perspectives align with our own, as it is only from a place of affection that we can responsibly and humanely support students in the learning process. Social justice is framed as a truly generative process, one that links mentors and learners in educational processes and calls upon us to adopt a pedagogy rooted in empathy, deep care, and commitment to those with whom we are involved in the learning process.

Social Justice 2.0 calls out the fact that while many of us have approached social justice work armed primarily with our values and personal commitment, in fact, we need more. Specifically, we need the appropriate tools to address the complex and nuanced world in which we live. We need not only knowledge and skills, but also the affective disposition to lovingly engage with the world and those with whom we are in educational relationship.

Advancing Social Justice provides essential guidance for redirection of social justice work on college and university campuses; it provides a context and framework that help us squarely and constructively address where we are at this point in our social justice efforts and approaches to redirect our work based on what the academy most needs from those of us who call ourselves educators. The book is theoretical, philosophical, and practical. It offers not only an orientation to the concept of social justice, but also guidance on how to initiate the process of adopting more socially just ways of teaching and leading.

Advancing Social Justice is a powerful call to action. This book is a thoughtful and well-articulated assessment of our approaches to social justice, with solidly grounded recommendations for moving forward. It will be of immense value in encouraging reflection among educators and challenging us to examine our beliefs and behaviors. *Advancing Social Justice* personally inspires me. This book not only is a guide to personal transformation but also maps the path to transforming our systems and processes. I will go even further and suggest that if we take the guidance of Davis and Harrison seriously, we have a blueprint for reclaiming the health of our campuses and restoring the spirits of so many whose lives have been negatively affected by social and institutional oppression. *Advancing Social Justice* makes an important and unique contribution to the conversation about the soul of higher education and the role educators play in fulfilling the grand promise of the academy.

Larry D. Roper
Vice provost for student affairs and
professor of ethnic studies
Oregon State University

Preface

This book is about theorizing and practicing social justice education differently. There are high-quality books that frame the issues surrounding social justice in higher education quite lucidly. Yet our experience with social justice education suggests that focusing on technical implementation of strategies has to give way to becoming and being socially just. The more we wrapped our heads around what we thought needed elucidation, the clearer it became that the model itself needed radical reexamination. It wasn't so much the concepts that needed reconsideration, but rather the processes or approaches that educators and those "in the know" use to promote learning and liberation.

We needed a shorthand way of talking about what we meant, which led one of us to start calling our idea "Social Justice 2.0." Working together on our iPads inspired this heuristic and helped us understand with greater clarity the book we wanted to write. Rather than simply adding new techniques to an existing paradigm of social justice education, we agreed with Steve Jobs's challenge to "think different." As with the iPad, we needed to create something that could shift our understanding of the nature of the work itself. We write as "friendly critics," people deeply committed to social justice both personally and professionally. Our critique comes from a place of serious concern about the future of social justice in higher education, not an indictment of it. We watch as diversity offices lose funding, affirmative action faces erosion, and hate incidents continue to proliferate, and we wonder if a fresh approach to how we theorize and articulate social justice in higher education is what is needed. We think it is.

What does Social Justice 2.0 look like? First, it questions what has become an unfortunate orthodoxy reminiscent of the very impulses that social justice educators tend to oppose in fundamentalist political approaches like those used by shock jocks and sound bite pundits. Too often, social justice education operates from the "getting it" model, dividing the world into enlightened students who agree with ideas like affirmative action or same-sex marriage and those who don't. As a result, the learning outcome becomes an indoctrination of sorts, which creates both confusion and resistance. Social Justice 2.0 rejects this notion of a neatly delineated left and right and right and wrong, proposing humility as the only workable starting place for truly engaging students in the intellectually and personally challenging work of social justice education. Humility can be terrifying for many reasons. Humility demands a vulnerability rarely achieved in intellectual spaces where making points and winning debates operate as currency. We propose that any movement forward in social justice education requires rethinking these academic economics.

At the same time, we argue for "meaning making" as the most effective starting point for social justice education. Sustaining social justice efforts requires a balancing of meaning-making capacities of the cognitive, intrapersonal, and interpersonal (Kegan, 1994). Instead of political correctness, then, the focus here is on academic correctness. That is, instead of constructing evidence to support one's political dogma, principles of critical theory and transformational learning guide interventions and actions. Learning that reflects on itself is the aim, or what Bateson (1991) calls *deutero learning*. Critical theorists, similarly, suggest using a constant focus of fundamental assumptions (especially related to power and economics) to deconstruct, contextualize, and recursively reexamine ideas in a manner that resists dogmatic stands in favor of staying awake to the complex interactions that our cognitive schemas too often ignore.

This is, in fact, how we define social justice—it is a means as much as an end. Too often, social justice is defined by *what* people do or believe; we would agree that actions and beliefs are elements of social justice. But the *how* is often the missing component. A person can hold good values like equality and fairness, yet fail to live up to the promise of social justice by demanding others accept his or her lens as "objective reality," painting all critics as oppressors, and/or failing to listen to alternative points of view. We argue for a definition of social justice that includes continual analysis of how people use power, including ourselves. Social justice education, then, is both substantive content and mindful process. It is the recursive illumination of institutional systems and personal biases that inhibit the equitable distribution of resources. And it also requires learning processes that uncover factors inhibiting the full and equal participation of all groups in society.

Another problematic way in which social justice tends to be defined is through the code of "good person cred." We do not oppose the desire to be good people, but we have observed on too many occasions how this phenomenon creates a political correctness paralysis of sorts, causing students and professors to police both themselves and others. In our experience, attempts at "being a good one" elicit behavioral modeling that leaves more deeply rooted consciousness unexamined. It also belies the reality that each of us, no matter how sophisticated, remains unfinished. If people in academic settings are not allowed to take intellectual risks and try out ideas without being accused of creating unsafe spaces, we risk replicating the same structural oppression we seek to challenge with concepts like academic freedom, free speech, and civil discourse. At its core, Social Justice 2.0 advocates a hard look at the paradigms and systems themselves with the aim of creating more effective means to the end of a sustainable social justice agenda.

A sustainable social justice agenda in the twenty-first century requires this shift for several reasons. First, paradigms that seek to indoctrinate leave social justice educators exposed to attacks from those who complain that higher education underrepresents conservative viewpoints. While we may disagree about whether there is a liberal bias in higher education, we can appreciate the points some critics make about the anti-intellectual impulses that allow some dogmas to be expressed while others are suppressed. We oppose arguments about balance, disagreeing with this as a goal since it would be almost impossible to reach consensus about where the center of an issue might lie. The points about indoctrination and dogma, however, resonate because academic environments must allow the free exchange of ideas regardless of how people feel about them. Retreating into arguments about safe spaces can undermine the intellectual enterprise at the core of any educational institution.

This is not to say that we believe safe spaces have no place in social justice education; in fact, our second reason for advocating Social Justice 2.0 deals directly with the role of emotion as inherent to any change process. Few would argue that social justice education doesn't push buttons; anger, fear, resistance, guilt, shame, and pain are just some of the feelings that students and educators experience as they wrestle with oppression, power, and privilege. To engage deeply with such charged topics, educators must create and hold a context that both challenges and supports students. Too often, students feel set up to fail when they are asked to share openly, but then feel attacked when they do so. Their natural response tends to be withdrawal, for which they are also confronted as an indicator of lack of willingness to own their issues. Part of the Social Justice 2.0 framework we espouse would take an honest look at this dynamic and find ways to reorient the pedagogical model itself toward a less polarizing, more generative approach. Parker Palmer

(2007) captured well the connection between the head and heart: "If you introduce a sudden stimulus to an unprepared person, the eyes narrow and the fight or flight syndrome kicks in. But if you train a person to practice soft eyes, then introduce that same stimulus, the reflex is often transcended. This person will turn toward the stimulus, take it in, and then make a more authentic response—such as thinking a new thought" (p. 116). Social Justice 2.0 begins from this position of "soft eyes," that is, a place of thinking and feeling as fundamentally inseparable processes. Creating safe spaces must extend beyond simply not saying things with which others might disagree into a place of the deeper mutual respect needed to begin any kind of meaningful dialogue. Moreover, we've found that institutional forces can bring both those targeted for and those privileged by oppression into the same conversation. A common focus where structural causes are explored can also illuminate different experiences (and related feelings of both guilt and anger) to begin a discussion of what needs to happen in order to achieve mutual liberation.

Our final reason for advocating Social Justice 2.0 relates to the structures of inequality that get us stuck in the first place. Shaun Harper (2008) offered an excellent example of this phenomenon in a national conference presentation in which he discussed an advertisement that garnered much attention for its racist portrayal. The ad for Intel features a white man standing amidst a group of black men bowing before him (to view the ad, go to http://www.visualnews.com/2010/12/18/tech-ads-that-got-their-plugs-pulled). During his talk, Harper made the point that the creator of this ad went through an educational system that failed to provide the critical thinking skills and awareness necessary to avoid reifying harmful stereotypes. As a result, there is now one more oppressive image in the world, adding to the already overwhelming number of routine ways in which marginalized people are negatively portrayed in our culture. Social Justice 2.0 asks us to both enlarge our screen to include greater consciousness of who is included and remember that technology is only as effective as the person who uses it.

Organization of the Book

Harper's story offers a powerful example of the dangerous cycle that can result when systems are not interrupted on a fundamental level. We must get to the essence to challenge deep-seated, ubiquitous, and taken-for-granted assumptions. In order to shift from vicious cycles to what Senge (1994) calls "virtuous circles," change has to occur at that most basic systemic level. This is why we begin in Chapter One with an analysis of how we know what we think we know. In this chapter, we posit epistemology as the most fundamental level for change. Positivist epistemological assumptions will continue to have us looking externally for objective truth that diminishes the salience of cultural, historical, and other contextual subjectivities that create and sustain injustice. Until we begin challenging how we know what we know we will continue to accept the terms of faulty systems and end up replicating them even in the process of trying to dismantle them.

Chapter Two serves to crystallize some of the concepts presented in the first chapter, demonstrating how they can serve as a toolkit of sorts for both educators and students. We suggest facility with these concepts as foundational knowledge for making sense of the ways in which privilege and oppression operate, sometimes despite our best efforts. Further, we advocate the contents of this toolkit as a common language for communicating across the incredible complexities that social justice education presents. In this chapter, we strive to provide both the theoretical and practical tools essential to move the social justice discourse forward.

In Chapter Three, we shift from the bigger picture of social justice generally to an examination of higher education's relationship with social justice (and injustice) historically. Effective social justice education begins with an acknowledgment of context, so we believe it is necessary to analyze how higher education institutions have served as vehicles for social justice and/or injustice. None of us operates in a vacuum, yet we sometimes fail to account for the forces that led to a particular conundrum. We seek to elucidate how the history of social justice in higher education continues to shape our social justice education practice in contemporary colleges and universities.

Chapters Four and Five name and address some of the pedagogical and personal challenges that arise for both educators and students participating in social justice education. Social justice educational content tends to confront our mental models and passively received knowledge, requiring alternative pedagogies that can help students manage the complexity of what they are learning. Chapter Four presents the principles of critical pedagogy, which can serve as useful strategies for introducing material that challenges conventional wisdom. Social justice educational content also presents conflicts on the emotional level, a topic addressed in Chapter Five. This chapter aims to assist social justice educators in troubleshooting tensions that naturally arise when institutional power, deeply held beliefs, and identity differences are negotiated. Everyone comes to this work with lived experiences rooted in personal identities and deeply held convictions about appropriate directions to achieve equity, inclusion, and social justice. Our goal in Chapter Five is to facilitate the process of reflecting on our own values and vulnerabilities so that we're not caught off guard in the heated discussions that can serve to either derail or enhance the educational process.

Chapters Six and Seven turn readers' attention to two vital but often overlooked knowledge bases for effective social justice education: media literacy and organizational theory. Chapter Six presents a Media Literacy 101 course of sorts, outlining key concepts and articulating their role as part of a comprehensive social justice curriculum. In Chapter Seven, we focus on the ways organizations themselves promote social injustice through hierarchical structures that centralize some while marginalizing others. We revisit notions of positivism and objective reality from previous chapters, showing how privilege and oppression can be mistaken for neutrality without an eye trained for seeing the ways systems reify the status quo. Frequently, we speak of "the system" in social justice circles without critically examining what systems are and how they operate. Both Chapters Six and Seven provide opportunities and strategies for unmasking the ideologies undergirding major institutions we take for granted in everyday life.

Chapter Eight concludes with an extension of this emphasis on strategy, providing theoretical and concrete ways to move social justice education to the next level. We employ Social Justice 2.0 as a positive, solution-focused way of addressing complex, nuanced twenty-first-century social justice conundrums. We do not suggest we are the first people to own any of these ideas, nor do we aim to characterize all the current social justice education work as "1.0." The technology metaphor can be extended here; we understand there will be bugs, patches, and newer versions required as our collective thinking about this complex topic evolves. We built this concept on a foundation developed by the many wise, compassionate people whose work we bring together in this book. We drew from interdisciplinary sources, both to add depth and richness to our ideas and to reflect the audience we imagined when writing this work.

Audience and Authors

Returning to the iPad as a metaphor, the tools we present ultimately belong to the people who will use them. We understand the iPad metaphor has its limits. Unlike the iPad, social justice is not a shiny toy one can take out of a box and start to use in a neat and orderly fashion. Who we are and our openness to the process of becoming are much more critical than where we stand or what tools we employ. A plumber without a wrench is weakened, but a plumber who does not know how to use a wrench should probably look for other employment.

While we both work as faculty in student affairs graduate preparation programs, we address this book broadly to faculty, practitioners, and students alike. We recognize the forces that have split our field into dichotomies such as student affairs or higher education, faculty or practitioners, educators or students. We believe these binaries are unhelpful to the educational enterprise, falsely and arbitrarily dividing what is naturally seamless. For example, student affairs work takes place in a higher education context, making the two fields interdependent both academically and politically. Similarly, faculty and practitioners affect one another in profound ways because we know students shift between the curricular and cocurricular multiple times through the day, learning and applying knowledge in both contexts. Finally, we know that in higher education as well as life more broadly, we're both teachers and students frequently, educating and learning from one another in ways far too complex for neat delineation.

Similarly, we position ourselves and readers as both teachers and learners, we do not envision active authors and passive readers, but strive to engage readers as participants through the use of critical questions and reflection opportunities throughout the work. Through these choices, we hope to model some ways in which the conventional lines that separate us might be blurred. So we shift the aforementioned "or" to an "and" sensibility, offering this work to academics and activists, faculty and practitioners, student affairs and higher education scholars, teachers and students. What distinguishes our audience is not the "who" or "what," but the "how." We write for those who, like us, struggle with the "how" of social justice education. How do we get unstuck and move social justice education forward in a way that resonates with people in the twenty-first century? How do we reach students and colleagues who think they've heard it all and have tuned out? How do we stay relevant when some social justice issues have confounded us for a long time? How do we keep from replicating the same systems we seek to change through social justice education? Ultimately, we wrote this book for those who, whatever their current position or field, seek fresh thinking about potential answers to these questions.

Acknowledgments

As with any scholarship we've published, this book is the result of numerous teachers who have provided stimulating insights, clarifying challenges, and nurturing compassion during our journey. Some, like bell hooks and Paulo Freire, have stimulated transformational learning through their ideas, while others have listened us into understanding. As important as mentorship and reading are, ultimately students are the ones who made this work possible. They've shared their stories, provided candid answers to what works or doesn't work in their social justice educational experiences, and stuck with us when we were trying to understand a cultural or personality difference, pushed too hard, or didn't listen deeply enough. We wish we had the space to name all the thoughtful, motivated, and inspiring students with whom we've had the privilege of connecting at Stanford, The University of Iowa, Western Illinois University, Ohio University, and the University of San Francisco. We'll have to trust that if you read this, you know we mean you.

Tracy Davis thanks his mentors, Debora Liddell and JQ Adams, who patiently listen, generously support, and appropriately challenge. Social justice is about being authentic, understanding who we are serving, quieting ego, being conscious of injustice in the world, and having the courage to risk—I can think of no better role models in my life than Deb and JQ. Over the years I have engaged in discussions with colleagues who have deepened my understanding of both the personal and institutional dimensions so critical to promoting equity and inclusion. I want to thank Rachel Wagner, Jason Laker, Bob Engel, Tim McMahon, Nicholas Colangelo, Alan Berkowitz, Rickey Hall, and Ron Pettigrew for introducing me to central concepts and walking beside me during critical times of frustration, misunderstanding, and the exultation of deepening consciousness. There are also colleagues at the Center for the Study of Masculinities and Men's Development whose insight, guidance, or friendship helped provide encouragement to complete this project. Thanks to Jim LaPrad, Sean Dixon, Burt Sorkey, Jennie Hemingway, Ron Williams, Keith Edwards, Vern Klobassa, Shaun Harper, Susan Marine, and Byron Oden Shabazz. I value Laura M. Harrison's wit, sense of humor, and collaborative style in writing this book and look forward to future projects. Finally, to Marjorie, Evan and Tyler: thank you for giving me space, sustenance, and support to explore and write. While the personal and professional are deeply intertwined in my work, you help me remember which is central.

Laura M. Harrison thanks her mentor and friend, Yegan Pillay, for his wise counsel and warm support, particularly during her transition to Ohio University. I don't know that I could have written my first book during my first year as faculty without the generous insight and encouragement I can always count on from him. I also want to acknowledge Patti Hanlon-Baker, Pete Mather, Gayle Yamauchi-Gleason, and Bob Young, whose guidance helped me get unstuck in writing, teaching, and life. My stories about their help continue to have a ripple effect as students hear them and realize it might be okay for them to reach out when they get stuck, too.

One of the fundamental strategies for promoting social justice discussed in this book is maintaining a dialectical disposition. This process of recursively challenging perspectives also reflects the way this book was written. The insightful blind reviewers' comments and John Schuh's expert questions and editing suggestions helped us clarify important details and reconsider the articulation of various viewpoints. Our editor, Erin Null, and assistant editor, Alison Knowles, were also instrumental in asking important questions and moving us through the writing process from inception to culmination. We would also like to thank readers who respond to our thoughts expressed in this book as we strive to maintain a dialectical disposition.

About the Authors

Tracy Davis is professor in the Department of Educational and Interdisciplinary Studies at Western Illinois University, where he also coordinates the College Student Personnel Program. In 2011 he began serving as director of the newly established Center for the Study of Masculinities and Men's Development. He has published widely regarding men's development, sexual assault prevention, and social justice. Davis coedited, for example, *Masculinities in Higher Education: Theoretical and Practical Considerations* with Jason Laker in 2011, coedited the 2013 *Critical Perspectives on Gender in Higher Education: An ASHE Reader*, and coauthored the *New Directions for Social Services* monograph *Developing Social Justice Allies*. His sexual assault prevention research has won numerous awards, including both the American College Personnel Association (ACPA) and National Association of Student Personnel Administrators (NASPA) outstanding dissertation award. Davis was also selected to the inaugural class of ACPA Emerging Scholars in 1999 and has received the ACPA Standing Committee for Men (SCM) Outstanding Research Award, the Commission on Student Development Assessment's Outstanding Assessment Article, and NASPA 2012 Men and Masculinities Knowledge Community Newly Published Research award. He was also selected as a 2013 ACPA Senior Scholar and received both the ACPA Annuit Coeptis award for Senior Scholars and the SCM Harry Canon Outstanding

Professional award in 2006. He is a frequent presenter, speaker, and consultant on college campuses. Most important, he remains wildly unfinished.

Laura M. Harrison began her career in student affairs as a practitioner at Ohio University, where she worked in residence life and lesbian, gay, bisexual, and transgendered (LGBT) programming. She moved to Stanford University in 2000, where she served as an associate dean of students, Women's Community Center director, resident fellow, and instructor in the Program in Feminist Studies. She also taught courses in leadership and change at the undergraduate, MBA, and doctoral levels at the University of San Francisco from 2006 to 2011. In 2011, she returned to Ohio University to accept the position she currently holds, assistant professor in the Counseling and Higher Education Department. Harrison teaches and writes on the topics of advocacy, change, and leadership in student affairs and higher education. The *Journal of Student Affairs Research and Practice, New Directions for Student Services,* and *Building Leadership Bridges Series* have published her work.

1

Uncovering Epistemology
Frameworks Supporting a Change Agenda

The problem is that most of us have spent our lives immersed in analytic knowing, with its dualistic separation of subject "I" and object "it." There's nothing wrong with analytic knowing. It's useful and appropriate for many activities—for example, for interacting with machines. But if it's our only way of knowing, we'll tend to apply it in all situations.
—Peter Senge (2008, p. 99)

Social justice education will stagnate if we do not challenge our prevailing assumptions about how we know what we think we know. According to Takacs (2002), "simply acknowledging that one's knowledge claims are not universal truths—that one's positionality can bias one's epistemology—is itself a leap for many people, one that can help to make us more open to the world's possibilities" (p. 169). Understanding epistemological frameworks helps us identify assumptions that we may take to be universal truths, just as failing to do so will leave us susceptible to our own limited point of view. Differing ways of knowing are deeply connected to our capacity to effect change. To be an effective change agent means something quite different if one believes truth is objective as opposed to subjective. Wineburg (2001) illustrates this when he states that "the narcissist sees the world—both the past and the present—in his own image. Mature historical knowing

1

teaches us to do the opposite: to go beyond our own image, to go beyond our brief life, and to go beyond the fleeting moment in history into which we have been born. When we develop the skill of understanding how we know what we know, we acquire a key to lifelong learning" (p. 24). We argue that unless we understand how we construct and shape knowledge, we risk reifying the status quo instead of promoting social justice. We can unwittingly work against our aims if we fail to understand our own lens with some degree of humility. Further, failure to acknowledge the subjective nature of knowledge can blind us to potential solutions that exist outside of our limited understanding of an issue. When we consider the common frustration regarding the persistent nature of some social justice issues, we have to wonder if part of the problem lies in failure to innovate, to address concerns in truly new ways that challenge interventions that have perhaps become obsolete.

My (Harrison's) motivation for exploring epistemology no doubt results from my previous job as the director of the Stanford Women's Community Center, where I strove to make advances for women. A big challenge in this career field stems from the reality that women have achieved legal equality and most people believe in gender equity, so the issues are less obvious than they were for people doing this kind of work fifty years ago. Yet concerns about sexism persist with regard to gender parity in higher education. Through my decade-plus experience doing women's advocacy work, it has become clear that the problems that remain in this area are rooted in epistemological concerns. The issue of underrepresentation of senior, tenured women faculty provides a good example of a concern in which a conventional understanding of the nature of knowledge has hindered change efforts. In a gesture undoubtedly motivated by goodwill and sincere desire to remedy a problem, many universities implemented "stop the tenure clock" policies so that women faculty would not be penalized for taking time off to have children. While the policy was helpful in many cases, the narrow focus on the tenure clock is not only limited, but counterproductive in some situations. For instance, if the prevailing paradigm of a department is that serious scholars achieve tenure in X number of years, then a professor faces significant political and professional repercussions for taking leave whether or not it is an official university policy to allow her to do so. In their groundbreaking study of male and female professors' career advancement, Mason, Wolfinger, and Goulden (2013) lauded tenure clock and other efforts aimed at creating more flexible policies for parents. But they also found that policies weren't enough; women continue to shoulder more of the parenthood responsibilities, and they pay the price professionally as a result. These conundrums do not mean a tenure clock policy is not useful; in fact, it may be a logical place to start. But it's not a good place to end: deeper, more substantive change requires the ability to examine what we think we know about academia, men, women, family, and work at their most basic levels.

Scholars have produced volumes of quality literature positing knowledge as a constructed social reality (Berger, 1966; Foucault, 1980; Habermas, 1973; Horkheimer, 1974; Marcuse, 1960). Distilling this literature is beyond the scope of this chapter; however, one goal here is to make the scholarship more accessible, because accessibility is an issue frequently acknowledged in the epistemological discourse (Tyson, 2006; Voronov & Coleman, 2003). The other primary aim of this chapter is to introduce participatory research as a methodological approach useful in addressing complex, long-standing social justice issues. What follows is an analysis of positivist versus postpositivist understandings of knowledge and an introduction to participatory research as an emancipatory epistemological tool. This chapter will explore participatory research's main concepts and analyze how this method can be applied to producing knowledge that yields fresh insights into what S. D. Parks (2005) called "swamp issues," the places where we get stuck.

Positivism versus Postpositivism

In a popular research textbook, Gall, Gall, and Borg (1999) define positivism as "an epistemological position that asserts that there is a social reality "out there" that is available for study through scientific means similar to those that were developed in the physical sciences" (p. 530). Positivism takes for granted that there is an objective reality that exists independently of contexts like cultural or power differences. Positivism does not deny the existence of culture or power, but it separates these as variables rather than lenses through which reality—and, by extension, knowledge—are constructed. In a positivist paradigm, reality is not constructed; it simply is. As a result, reality is to some degree stagnant because it does not change as the result of our interaction with it. Reality and knowledge exist outside of ourselves in a positivist worldview. We interact with them, to be sure, but *we* and *them* are separate entities.

In contrast, postpositivism takes issue with the idea of a baseline reality that transcends difference, particularly differences related to culture and/or power. In a postpositivist framework, reality itself is understood as constructed, which raises questions about the *constructor*. For example, who has access to education, and are there differences in the quality of educational experience based on who the learner is? Postpositivists tend to acknowledge that the level of access to the construction materials varies according to power; people exist in relation to other people via various hierarchies, even in the flattest of organizations. Position title, where people went to school, level of education attained, political involvement, and family connections are just some of the potential criteria for establishing privilege or marginalization within an institution. Is there a relationship, for example, between ethnicity and educational resources at the primary or secondary school level? Imagining that these distinctions would not affect who gets to define the dominant discourse that shapes educational policy seems illogical, yet the default objective assumption is that there is indeed some sort of power-free, context-free knowledge that prevails purely through its intrinsic merit. Greenfield and Ribbins (1993) suggested a way to examine how power affects the way knowledge is constituted:

> We should look more carefully too for differences in objectives among different kinds of people in organizations and begin to relate these to differences in power or access to resources. Although this concept of organization permits us to speak of the dominating demands and beliefs of some individuals, and allows us to explore how those with dominating views use the advantage of their position, we need not think of these dominating views as "necessary," "efficient," "satisfying," or even "functional," but merely as an invented social reality, which holds true for a time and is then vulnerable to redefinition through changing demands and beliefs among people [p. 17].

The difference between a positivist and postpositivist understanding of knowledge has important, real-world implications. If we return to the tenure clock example, the creation and implementation of this policy using a positivist approach limits the possibility for understanding the issue in its full complexity. In this framework, the problem is that women need time off to have children and should receive additional leave to do so. If the policy does not solve the problem, the institution can conduct a survey or tinker with the amount of time that might be needed, but the deeper problem is likely to remain intact. In a postpositivist frame, the construction of the problem in the first place is on the table. How reality itself is defined is called into question, with inquiries such as, Why is parental leave framed as a women's issue? Certainly there is no way around the fact that the actual birthing falls to women, but there is no natural law mandating that mothers must serve as primary caregivers. In a postpositivist frame, the issue of what it means to accomplish meaningful work might also be examined. Does work have to happen between the hours of 9 a.m. and 5 p.m. in an office, five days a week? The nature of work would also likely be called into question. Why is some work valued (that is, paid work like teaching) and other work considered "leave" (that is, bearing and raising the next generation)? The argument could certainly be made that we live in an overpopulated world and do not desire to make it easy for people to raise families. This would no doubt be a controversial claim, but it would be an honest one that acknowledges an ideology, unlike the current situation in which people give lip service to being "family-friendly" or sup- porting "work-life balance," while allowing institutional policies and practices that do not align with these values. Policy discussions born of a postpositivist approach would ask deeper questions about the institutional culture, allowing for the kind of substantive critique necessary as a precursor to meaningful change.

Postpositivism and Context

In a similar vein to the tenure clock example, Giroux (2001) contrasts how a positivist epistemological framework might limit one's understanding of a seemingly simple phenomenon such as disparate productivity rates between two groups of workers: "For instance, an empirical study that concludes that native workers in a colonized country work at a slower rate than imported workers who perform the same job may provide an answer that is correct, but such an answer tells us little about the domination or the resistance of workers under its sway. That the native workers may slow down their rate as an act of resistance is not considered here. Thus, the notions of intentionality and historical context are dissolved within the confines of a limiting quantifying methodology" (pp. 16–17). Giroux's (2001) example articulates the multiple vantage points from which something that looks like an uncomplicated difference in worker output could be constructed differently depending on the research method applied. Simple measurement would produce knowledge about the differences between the two groups, but a method capable of capturing more complexity would be necessary to elucidate the deeper issues at play. Most important, this example demonstrates the importance of context in understanding complex phenomena. Because a postpositivist worldview does not separate reality, knowledge, and context, a more complete picture of what is really happening in a specific situation is possible.

Specificity is an important dimension of postpositivism's potential role in a social justice–oriented approach to knowledge production. Because postpositivist models do not acknowledge an objective reality that can transcend culture or power differences, they do not strive for generalizability. As a result, they avoid the "one-size-fits-all" pitfall underlying much of both the faulty knowledge claims and poor policy that lie beneath many of the social injustices that persist. Failure to examine a phenomenon in depth often leads to theorizing that reduces it in ways that diminish its complexity. This tendency leads to attempts at universal truth claims, which very quickly gloss over realities invisible to the majority understanding of a situation. Edward Said (2002) described this issue as the universal eclipsing the local, creating a situation where what counts as real or true is simply the point of view of those in power.

The good news is that postpositivist paradigms make it possible to negotiate so-called objective reality in a way impossible under a positivist worldview. By challenging normativity at its core, disability studies scholars provide excellent examples of the relationship between epistemology and social justice, such as this one, regarding a community with a high percentage of deafness: "The deaf people who lived there at the time did not live in a disabling society because everyone learned to use sign language. A person in a wheelchair is only disabled if there is no cut in the sidewalk or elevator in a multistory building" (Mertens, Sullivan, & Stace, 2011, p. 228). Instead of focusing on the ways in which individuals may fail to conform to assumptions underlying communities or architecture, disabilities studies scholars emphasize how the ideas about both "disability" and "normalcy" are constructed in these environmental contexts. Seen from another perspective, the disability is not with the person, but in the environment. The liberatory potential for what can seem like a subtle difference is enormous because contexts are changeable in ways that "objective reality" is not.

Postpositivism versus Relativism

Postpositivism provides the intellectual basis for knowledge construction that emancipates in many contexts. There is a risk, however, in confusing postpositivism with radical relativism, which some use to justify a values-free approach to knowledge. This is admittedly slippery territory; what I find to be a universal human right, for example, may differ very much from someone else's. Our differences may very well exist due to variations in our culture and/or positions of power. Stanford political theorist Susan Okin (1999) provided one of the better examples of how truly complex this issue is in her book *Is Multiculturalism Bad for Women?* I (Harrison) started at Stanford the year after this book was published and experienced the angst this book caused for progressive people, who wanted to support both multiculturalism and feminism. Postpositivism has played an important role in social justice movements, especially feminism, where scholars and activists alike have pointed out the ways in which essentialist notions of masculinity and femininity have caused limitations for both men and women. Yet postpositivism can be conflated with a radical relativism of sorts, leading some to question whether it's acceptable to critique almost any cultural belief or practice. Okin (1999) articulates this tension well: "Those who practice some of the most controversial such customs—clitoridectomy, the marriage of children or marriages that are otherwise coerced, or polygamy—sometimes explicitly defend them as necessary for controlling women, and openly acknowledge that the customs persist at men's insistence" (p. 14). The line is unclear, to be sure. Feminists and multicultural activists alike—many of whom span both worlds—disagree on many of these conflicts. Some advocate for a more universal understanding of human rights that would include a ban on a practice like clitoridectomy; others argue that working within cultures to ensure a safer and more humane approach to this custom is the better course of action. It's easy to knee-jerk into statements on either end of the spectrum; "that's just wrong" and "it's their culture" are frequently stated, yet rarely helpful.

To be honest, a topic like clitoridectomy sends me (Harrison) straight into a positivist mindset because I find the idea horrifying. I struggle with this as both a feminist and a person committed to multiculturalism. This was a "swamp issue" for me, a place where I felt stuck. Fortunately, I became close enough to a student from Ethiopia to have the rapport necessary to ask her what she thought about this practice. She explained to me that she was against it, but that I had to understand that the horror I felt was also culture-bound. She compared the situation to her reaction to seeing her first anorexic women in the United States and feeling completely disturbed by the idea that someone would willingly starve herself. This student helped me understand that while I, too, find anorexia problematic, I react less to it as something sadly more normal in my culture. She told me that the first time she saw a dangerously thin woman, she wanted to shove a hamburger into the woman's mouth, a similar impulse toward the force I would want to use to stop clitoridectomy. We agreed these would not be the most effective interventions and that deeper, more substantive change would require truly understanding the contexts that produced both behaviors, including colonialism, which was a connection I had not made before. Fortunately, participatory research exists as a more intentional way to get to the place where I had the good fortune to arrive with the help of my student. It does not solve the problem of determining exactly where the line between positivism and postpositivism ought to be with respect to social justice issues, but it does provide a method for getting to the deeper knowledge needed to get unstuck and effect change more thoughtfully.

Participatory Research as a Model for Knowing

Participatory research is more of an approach to understanding knowledge than a specific set of techniques, though it does offer concrete methodological tools we will discuss later. At its core, participatory research exists in opposition to traditional research in three important ways. First, as an extension of the idea of knowledge as constructed, participatory research does not seek to separate the researcher from the researched, understanding both parties as two (or more) active agents in an iterative process, rather than the traditional notion of a scholar doing research *on* or *to* a subject. Second, participatory researchers conduct inquiry in a way that reunites the dichotomized ideas of theory and practice, aiming for knowledge born of application and a lived experience informed by sound theory. Third, and perhaps most important, participatory research seeks an emancipatory end. In its understanding of knowledge as something that cannot be values-neutral, researchers using a participatory framework do not seek a values-free end. Each of these points presents a counternarrative to the dominant discourse about how knowledge is produced and consumed and therefore warrants further exploration in the sections that follow.

Co-Researchers

Understanding knowledge as constructed provides the philosophical basis for the radical reexamination of the researcher-subject paradigm. Rather than conceptualizing people as subjects on whom to conduct research, participatory approaches treats people as active agents in the construction of knowledge. By naming the taken-for-granted ways in which traditional research is carried out, Kieffer (1981) unmasks the power dynamic created and reinforced in this hegemonic relationship, explaining, "As long as the academic researcher initiates contact, negotiates refinement, selects participants, carries out procedures, chooses the focus of interpretation, and owns the results, the inequities of power continue to exist. A participatory framework makes normally hidden relations of power explicit and engages the participants, post-hoc, in personal ownership. It surrenders control of information and consciously draws them in to interpretation" (p. 5).

By conceptualizing those viewed as subjects in traditional research as participants, participatory research allows for a more equitable understanding of knowledge production as a collaborative process. In a similar manner, the inclusion of participants not only in the data collection stage, but in the analysis process as well, allows them to participate more fully in the process of generating new knowledge. But, most important, the simple act of repositioning the researcher and participants as equals stimulates a meaningful counternarrative about the nature of knowledge as more subjective than objective.

Breaking the boundaries between researcher and researched is difficult, making the co-researcher model an "easier said than done" prospect at times. Smith, Bratini, Chambers, Jensen, and Romero (2010) write eloquently about the challenges of restructuring the research relationship in a way that is truly equitable. In a situation where researchers and participants were asked simply to introduce themselves, Jensen shared the following reflection: "In the moment that I was asked to participate in that same discussion with participants, I was struck with an anxiety-provoking realization. It was easy to say to my colleagues at school that I wanted to help and advocate for queer youth in our city. However, to say 'I want to help you' to a group of people who were actually more comfortable with their sexuality than I was seemed incredibly presumptuous. Immediately, I realized I was still not viewing the organization's members as equal partners in the project" (p. 411).

This example also helps illustrate how the co-researcher paradigm could be extended to mitigate power differences between professors and/or student affairs professionals and students. Rather than defaulting to the position of professor or student affairs professional as active agent and student as passive participant, making this shift in one's mind has the potential to transform one's pedagogy and/or practice. If you view your educator role in a participatory manner, how do you listen differently? Do you make more or fewer statements, ask more or fewer questions? What kinds of questions do you ask? Both parties benefit from this more egalitarian approach, which fosters creativity and therefore expanded possibilities for innovation, particularly with regard to social justice issues. This shift also creates greater congruence by not only teaching about social justice as a topic, but demonstrating it in one's approach to students.

Because of the democratic nature of the knowledge construction process in participatory research, it requires reflection and self-examination on the part of all parties involved. Smith, Bratini, Chambers, Jensen, and Romero (2010) pointed out that this was true for the participants as well, who had internalized the dominant culture's explanations for their perceived shortcomings. Conventional research in which an expert extracts data from passive subjects is likely easier and more efficient in many ways. But it also fails to capture phenomenological complexity by failing to ensure the researcher's worldview is not simply replicated in the data analysis. As a result, the co-researcher design in participatory research increases the likelihood of producing truly new knowledge by accounting for the inevitable ways researchers influence knowledge production.

Praxis

Another way in which participatory research facilitates fresh and creative knowledge is by using the conceptual tool, praxis, to break down the theory-practice dichotomy. Coined by Paolo Freire

(1970), *praxis* is defined as "reflection and action upon the world in order to transform it" (p. 36). This change mandate inherent to participatory research enhances its utility as a methodology appropriate for negotiating complexity. Change is not a new focus in the literature on complexity; in fact, one could argue convincingly that change defines the complexity discourse. Yet conventional epistemologies are disinclined to champion any sort of change agenda in research, opting for some sort of scholarly distance that tends to dull the research's more interesting edges. As an aside, the recent proliferation of scholars criticizing the uselessness of much academic research (for example, Hacker & Dreifus, 2010) might be mitigated if more researchers employed methodologies that embraced rather than eschewed practical application. Participatory research reunites the unnecessarily separated ideas of theory and practice, adding to its appeal as a methodology up to the task of enabling change by endorsing both lived experience and empirical data as legitimate sources of knowledge.

Praxis helps focus the lens in determining what merits study. In traditional epistemologies where there is believed to be a consensus about what is objective or normal, what typically warrants investigation is whatever is perceived as outside of this frame. When theory is born of lived experience rather than a constructed idea of what might be novel, greater possibilities open. Forester (1999) offers an excellent example: "When we examine it, ordinary action turns out to be extraordinarily rich. What passes for 'ordinary work' in professional-bureaucratic settings is a thickly layered texture of political struggles concerning power and authority, cultural negotiations over identities, and social constructions of the 'problems' at hand" (p. 47). Here, Forester demonstrates why the ordinary is worth studying; that is, there is a normally hidden process by which something becomes collectively understood as ordinary. The expression "taken for granted" is most often used passively or as an adjective, but it is essentially an active process to "take something for granted." Seeing what our minds accept as objective reality or ordinary poses an intellectual challenge, much like the proverbial fish in water that only understands it is in water when pulled out of the tank and thrust into the air. Duberley and Johnson (2011) discuss negation as a tool "to challenge what is taken for granted as the natural order of things and to see things that are assumed to be rational and ordinary as exotic" (p. 351). Negation creates the possibility of defamiliarizing ourselves with our taken-for-granted assumptions about what constitutes normalcy so that we can see it with a fresh set of eyes. As is the case for the fish suspended outside the only environment it has ever known, negation is likely to cause discomfort. Yet negation offers a vital first step in effecting change; that is, exposing something that appears to be a natural law as, in fact, constructed and therefore changeable.

Expanding the parameters for what can be changed allows for truly novel inquiry. Ada and Beutel (1993) wrote about the utility of participatory research methods for researchers exploring fairly uncharted territory: "The challenge and richness you will face as a researcher doing participatory research is that of identifying, naming, and giving voice to knowledge that is not yet codified or legitimated by the dominant society. It is the nature of participatory research to intentionally go after knowledge that is not traditionally part of the already established and published store of knowledge" (p. 11). Praxis expands conventional ideas about what is worthy of study by blurring the line between subject and object. This is similar to the ways in which participatory research makes the relationship between researcher and researched more hazy than in conventional knowledge production. As with interdisciplinarity, these facets extend the frontiers of knowledge in ways that more reductive structures tend to stifle with their disciplinary boxes and discrete categories.

Emancipation

Participatory research is a methodology, a means to an end. What has been discussed so far is its role as a means, but what really drove its creation is the idea propagating a positive end. *Positive* in this case is not some sort of benignly general idea; the positive end sought in participatory research is clearly social justice focused in its mission. Participatory research advances a democratic aim, seeking to broaden the true participation from which it gets its name. More specifically, participatory research aims to redistribute life chances through demonstrating how positivist epistemologies are complicit in reflecting and creating unjust hierarchies.

Hierarchy presents an interesting example of how the way in which knowledge is constructed has a concrete impact on organizational life. Conventional wisdom states that hierarchy is a good thing, that it is a necessary feature in institutions in order to prevent chaos, foster accountability, and promote efficiency. Yet Child (2011) presents a powerful counternarrative to this idea: "Hierarchy creates a relational distance between people. It lends itself to information asymmetry, lack of transparency, and low mutual understanding. The agency problem in hierarchies can consequently operate in both directions, with senior management failing to secure the commitment of those in lower positions and the latter not being able to constrain or expose malpractice at the top. The distance between controllers and controlled has increased along with the rise of megacorporations and government departments" (pp. 508–509).

Some will advocate hierarchy's merits as a means toward efficiency. But the question must always be asked about efficiency to what end. Too often, efficiency is described in neutral terms rather than acknowledging that what is seen as central or marginal in the efficiency process is often privilege-laden. Hierarchy is an enticing idea, particularly when one has benefited from hierarchical ways of organizing that privilege his or her way of thinking. It's easy to mistake both what one senses as urgent and what tasks and people are peripheral for objective reality. Participatory research aims to name and remedy this problem by highlighting the limits of linearity itself, exposing its hidden political dimension.

In its dismantling of hierarchies between researcher and researched and theory and practice, participatory research takes aim at hierarchies between the powerful and the powerless as well. Not content to simply give voice to the paradigms of those in power, participatory research refuses the "disinterested researcher" stance. Interest in effecting positive change very much drives participatory research, making it a frequent site for emancipatory action based on new understandings of what constitutes legitimate knowledge.

Some scholars argue that participatory research does not go far enough in promoting concrete change initiatives (Kinsler, 2010). This argument has merit, but we caution against underestimating the power of theory. The way we think produces real-world outcomes that impact people's lives. Even the discourse on change itself provides an excellent example. The current zeitgeist endorses a very cheery narrative about change, but Morgan and Spicer (2011) present an alternative perspective: "The result is change becomes a ubiquitous phenomenon that has no boundary ... they (critics) remind us that our fluid and flexible working lives have produced heightened anxiety, a pervasive sense of insecurity, the destruction of common bonds, and the destruction of livelihoods and ways of life across the world" (pp. 251–252). An uncritical acceptance of the current change discourse presents real dangers. Change that comes after an inclusive process where voices of those affected by it are carefully heard and seriously considered builds relationships and reduces anxiety, even if not all parties get everything they want. For example, organizational power brokers frequently dismiss substantive objections to new austerity measures as simple "resistance to change." A postpositivist epistemology exposes change as not a neutral phenomenon: there are changes that emancipate and processes that reflect integrity that should be implemented, and there are changes and methods that oppress and ought therefore to be resisted. Changes that neither emancipate nor oppress undoubtedly exist, but they are fewer than the contemporary change discourse acknowledges.

Conclusion

In this chapter, we propose participatory research as an episte-mological framework that supports a change agenda. A complex world demands a sophisticated epistemology that illuminates the interests, structures, and systems at work in the complicated orga-nizations that define contemporary existence. Few would argue that our complex world does not need change; growing environ-mental degradation, poverty, corruption, and intolerance offer just a few examples that illustrate flaws in the current course. Many people desire change, yet change proves elusive because our ways of knowing lead us to replicate the same thinking that got us into a problem in the first place.

Alvesson, Bridgman, and Willmott (2011) argue that our col-lective inability to challenge the status quo in any substantive way hamstrings potentially meaningful change efforts: "The natural and legitimate nature of the dominant social order is taken for granted and problems are seen as minor or moderate imperfections to be resolved or, when not, are seen to be unavoidable. Broader and deeper ethical and political issues and questions—such as the distribution of life chances within corporations or the absence of any meaningful democracy in working life—are either ignored or, at best, marginally accommodated through, for example, pro-grammes of employee 'involvement' and 'consultation'" (p. 10). The aforementioned picture is bleak, but organizational life does not necessarily have to be so. Postpositivist epistemologies demon-strate that there is no natural law stating that organizations must operate on hierarchical models. Participatory research offers a way to excavate the new knowledge needed to fuel truly creative alter-natives to the thinking that created the situation in which we now find ourselves. What we experience as reality is simply the current construction; an alternative methodology enables change. New means can yield new ends.

2

A Toolkit for Understanding a Social Justice Paradigm

America, in the assembly of nations, has uniformly spoken among them the language of equal liberty, equal justice and equal rights.

—John Quincy Adams

America is exceptional because, unlike any other nation, it is dedicated to the principles of human liberty, grounded on the truths that all men are created equal and endowed with equal rights. These permanent truths are "applicable to all men and all times," as Abraham Lincoln once said.

—Matthew Spalding (2010, p. 11)

U nderstanding the complexities in Chapter One regarding epistemology is central to developing a social justice pedagogy and practice. Unless we are open to excavating the assumptions about *how* we know *what* we know, we will not generally ask the fundamental and often hidden questions necessary for uncovering systems of injustice. In addition to comprehending the impact of epistemology, we have found an array of vital concepts related to implementing social justice praxis. Over the past two decades we have participated in a higher education discourse regarding issues related to social justice. We have taught classes focusing on identity dimensions of race, class, sexual orientation, spirituality, and gender in the context of systematic oppression. We have each served as director of a center focused on gender where we participated in both research and service aimed at promoting equity and justice. We've discovered that in our classrooms, conferences, professional offices, and other sites of engagement around social justice, terminology and meanings associated with various concepts can either advance understanding or reduce discussions to ego-enlisting debates. The difference often involves "land-mine" language, where someone reacts to another based on their history with a word, rather than exploring the possibility of multiple meanings or even intent. We believe it is incumbent on education professionals to engage in scholarly questioning when confronted with language that they deem offensive or otherwise inappropriate. Too often, we have witnessed educators engaging in what a colleague of ours calls "taking inventory" (R. Wagner, personal communication, March 27, 2011). She suggests that education professionals are often quick to judge the way someone behaves and to assess their racism, sexism, homophobia, or other form of oppression. Ironically, taking inventory in this way not only distances us in a manner that inhibits learning, but it also represents a hypocritical failure in realizing that we have all held biases, socialized oppression affects us all, and that we are all unfinished.

Rather than viewing sexist or racist remarks as opportunities to correct people, educators should see them as invitations to engage in discussion in order to cocreate learning. The kind of policing of expression that simply exchanges allegedly inappropriate terms with more politically correct language fails as a learning practice and simply replaces one dogma with another. Laker (2003), for example, developed the phrase "bad dogging" to describe how some educators wag their metaphorical fingers in shame at potentially harmful behaviors in a way that both releases the accuser from engaging the accused in a deeper learning process and teaches the accused to simply avoid such language or behavior in front of the accuser. As one of our professors in graduate school taught us, we should be more concerned about *academic correctness* than *political correctness*. That is, we should use processes of inquiry that follow academic guidelines, like using evidence, and pedagogy that further encourages people to reach their own conclusions. Do you recognize the difference in your engagement when you are seeking to be right as opposed to seeking understanding? Academic correctness is concerned with one's familiarity with the scholarship on the topic of discussion, an awareness of how epistemology and methods of inquiry affect so-called facts, openness to and awareness of evidence that contradicts one's stance, and consideration of complex contextual influences.

Defining Social Justice

With regard to social justice, an initial step toward the scholarly engagement of discourse is to define terms. Equal liberty, equal justice, and equal rights are fundamental to U.S. democracy, as outlined by our founding fathers, reinforced by leaders since, and illustrated in the quotes at the beginning of this chapter. Few would argue with these aims, but how does one define "equal," who gets to decide, and how would one assess whether or not we are achieving this critical mission? In order to evaluate whether or not our actions are congruent with these aims, we need to assemble a toolkit to help us discern the complexities associated with social justice. In other words, to measure the integrity of our democratic system expressed clearly in the Declaration of Independence and U.S. Constitution, and touted as the structural foundation for the critical fundamental principles that make America exceptional, we need a means to measure both the procedures used and the outcomes realized related to these principles. Justice and equal rights require fair processes that offer equal opportunities for successful pursuit of life, liberty, and happiness. As Tornblom and Vermunt (2007) suggest, an overall assessment of the fairness of a situation requires information about outcomes (distributive justice), as well as the processes by which the outcomes were produced (procedural justice). Thus, one definition of social justice is the equitable processes and outcomes that result from efforts to close the gap between what we espouse in our social contract and how we actually enact such a mission. Another definition, congruent with the first and providing a little more specificity, is Bell's (2007) articulation of social justice as the "full and equal participation of all groups in a society that is mutually shaped to meet their needs. Social justice includes a vision of society in which the distribution of resources is equitable and all members are physically and psychologically safe and secure ... The process for attaining the goal of social justice ... should be democratic and participatory, inclusive, and affirming of human agency and human capacities for working collaboratively to create change" (pp. 1–2).

It follows from these definitions that social justice is an attempt to establish integrity between mission and action.

Social justice actions, then, are actions designed to remove hurdles to equal opportunity, equal rights, and human liberty. So far, it seems that there should be little controversy over the aims and definitions of social justice. What could be controversial about asking that the processes used and outcomes realized are congruent with the articulated mission statement of this country? For example, the unequal treatment of soldiers returning from World War II based on ethnicity (see Chapter Three) illustrates processes that conflicted with equal rights promised in the U.S. Constitution. Passage of the Civil Rights Act and subsequent enforcement of the laws were acts of social justice whereby some gaps between our *espoused* mission in the country and the *enacted* mission were bridged. However, in contemporary society and higher education, social justice is anything but simple and is in fact currently highly controversial. For example, the National Council for Accreditation of Teacher Education (NCATE), facing pressure from conservative groups, dropped the terms "social justice" from its list of teacher candidate dispositions that included beliefs and attitudes including caring, fairness, honesty, and responsibility (Wasley, 2006). Claims that social justice "has political overtones and can be used by institutions to weed out would-be teachers based on their social and political beliefs" (p. A13) are based in fear, not evidence—fear that policies and practices will no longer favor some individuals over others. Readers should consider whether there is evidence substantiating the claim that political and social beliefs have prevented teachers from getting jobs. In fact, equal protection laws and the concept of academic freedom are specifically designed to prevent such bias. If social justice, as we have here defined it, means working to ensure that our policies, practices, and procedures are congruent with our constitutional protections of equal opportunity, can anyone seriously imagine a teacher saying, "You know, I'm not sure I can believe in equal protection for all and, moreover, policies that are aimed at ensuring equal rights are wrong"? The reason social justice language is challenged has to do with the unarticulated fear that raising consciousness about the disparities that still exist between mission and actuality will threaten the status quo—a status quo that currently advantages those in power.

In addition to the fear of losing benefits that are sustained by maintaining the status quo, we believe that a lack of common language and a complex social justice conceptual framework undermines accuracy and clarity in the discourse about social justice. In this chapter we attempt to make sense of these complications by providing scaffolding for readers to use in mindfully analyzing the social justice landscape in higher education. We will discuss an array of definitions, meanings, and central concepts that illuminate how people become plugged in to the matrix of hegemony and learn fundamental assumptions that make seeing the need for social justice obscure. Just as some readers may have been surprised by some historical facts that were withheld from the curriculum, some will likely be similarly shocked at how processes of oppression and what Herman and Chomsky (1998) call "manufacturing of consent" remain hidden. In fact, we will illustrate throughout this book how acculturation to certain norms and the nature of privilege coalesce to not only blind many to the systems of oppression, but also build resistance to concepts, discussions, and lived experiences that reflect such influences.

Equity versus Equality

The difference between the concepts of equity and equality illustrates how "common-sense knowledge" can mask critical distinctions so important to understanding a social justice perspective. While equity and equality are often treated as synonyms, the implications that the differences have in promoting social justice are profound. *Equality* suggests that everyone should be treated the same, regardless of background, history, or needs. *Equity*, on the other hand, takes into account historical disadvantages, human diversities, and potentially unique needs. This distinction is critical because policies that treat people uniformly may actually represent processes that result in unjust outcomes. For example, a first-generation Latino female with a learning disability and coming from an underfunded school district represents a radically different experience in education from a fourth-generation, African American, gay male from an upper-class background who attended private school. A simple undifferentiated category of "other" in determining admissions, scholarships, or any educational policy will fail to address the kind of individualized attention that promoting learning and development require. According to Zine (2001), "if we want to truly service the needs of diverse communities and create inclusive spaces for community involvement in education, then it is imperative to create specifically focused policies, goals and initiatives which will do justice to all groups striving for equity" (p. 259). While equal treatment is an efficient strategy for implementing institutional policies with an illusion of fairness, it fails miserably as an educational strategy congruent with the intended mission of equitable opportunity in this democracy.

Patton, Shahjahan, and Osei-Kofi (2010) argue that oppression does not homogenize groups of marginalized people, but affects individuals with different constellations of identities, histories, and contexts differentially. A policy or practice that ignores such realities will fall short of providing equitable opportunity. As Lee (1999) suggests, "the goal is not equality where everyone gets the same amount of the pie. It's equity, where people get what they need" (p. 23). These scholars call into question educational practices and policies that treat students the same. As educators, we can testify to the varying advising and pedagogical strategies necessary for different students in a whole host of contexts. For example, keynote addresses, one-on-one advising, and classroom teaching each call for different learning approaches. Similarly, past educational experiences and varying social backgrounds bring students to college with different learning needs, expectations, and goals. Indeed, teaching the same material to different groups of students is always unique. Just as plumbers use different tools to address different plumbing needs, it should not be asking too much for educational practices and policies to account for the different needs of students who come to our campuses. We agree with Zine (2001), who argues that true equity "goes deeper than protecting a sense of vested self-interest with regard to personal or collective rights; it speaks to the need to develop more fine grained sociological and practical equivalents to what the values of equality, justice and respect for diversity actually mean in the real world of identity politics and educational praxis" (p. 250). Thus, we need to interrogate the one-size-fits-all policies and practices that obscure human differences, systems of oppression, history, and institutional contexts that lead to illusions of equality at the cost of genuine equity.

So far we have seen how social justice is complicated by fear and its effective realization muddled by superficial conceptualizations of fairness in terms of equality rather than equity. In order to engage in a more rigorous, critical, and thoughtful discussion about social justice in higher education, it is important to also acquire (a) a well-defined set of terms, (b) a clear understanding of the participants in higher education with regard to who they are and how they make meaning, and (c) a firm grasp of how organizational systems and social conditions influence the individuals for whom educational outcomes are aimed. Our theoretical framework, in other words, is grounded in a constructivist perspective that reality is cocreated through interactions between self and environment. In order to appreciate both the need for and the practice of social justice, it is essential to understand that the self is multidimensional and identity is intersectional. It is simultaneously critical to connect individual identities with the social milieu where structural oppression is institutionalized and identities are coconstructed through experiences of domination and subordination. After elucidating a number of key concepts, then, we will describe both the social construction of identities and the structural systems of oppression, which we hope will illuminate why we need social justice–focused education today. As you will see in the historical struggles described in Chapter Three, developing strategies to maintain an inclusive, fair, and equitable democracy will not be a simple achievement.

Critical Definitions

Exhibit 2.1 presents a list of terms that have proven helpful to students and others with whom we've engaged in discussions of social justice. In the spirit of academic correctness, our intent is not to provide an exhaustive or even absolutely correct list of terms. The ever-changing and dynamic nature of language and the constructed nature of reality itself inhibit the establishment of terms and definitions that are "true" once and for all. Rather, it is critical to treat these terms as sites of engagement, debate, and reconstruction if necessary. We encourage a broad and continuing dialogue about which terms are essential, which should be dropped, what concepts need to be added, and which concepts need clarifying or redefining. Since language is dynamic, contextual, and often contains subtext and/or multiple meanings, it stands to reason that we seek understanding rather than seeking only one reality. This sort of paradox, where we need both the possibility of multiple meanings and a shared language, motivates us to offer the list in Exhibit 2.1.

Exhibit 2.1. A Common Language for Discussing Social Justice

Note: The references cited here are listed at the end of this exhibit.

Ableism   Discrimination against people with disabilities in favor of people who are (perceived to be) able-bodied (Reason, Broido, Davis, & Evans, 2005).

Acculturation   The exchange of cultural features that results when groups of individuals having different cultures come into continuous first-hand contact; the original cultural patterns of either or both groups may be altered, but the groups remain distinct (J. Q. Adams, 2003).

Agent group   A group of people who are socialized and conditioned to perpetrate oppression (Reason et al., 2005).

Ally   Someone from the agent group who will "stand in the way" of oppression when it is aimed at a target person; someone who will recognize privilege as a member of the agent group and will question and resist the institutionalized oppression as much as possible. An ally is most effective at fighting oppression when he or she realizes that it hurts both the target group members and the agent group members (Reason et al., 2005).

Assimilation   The process whereby a minority group gradually adapts to the customs and attitudes of the prevailing culture (J. Q. Adams, 2003).

Constructivism   An epistemological position that affirms that learning is an active process where people actively create their own subjective representations of objective reality. It identifies knowledge as a process where new information is linked to prior knowledge and mental representations are subjective (Kincheloe, 2005).

Counternarratives   Stories of individuals and groups whose narratives have been marginalized, lost, skewed, or remain untold. These narratives challenge dominant discourses that serve to target some and protect others from oppression.

(continued)

(continued)

Dialectic   Proposes that knowledge is not complete in and of itself. It is produced in a larger process and can never be understood outside of its historical development and its relationship to other information (Kincheloe, 2005).

Discourse analysis   A study in which a discourse is defined as a constellation of hidden historical rules that govern what can be and cannot be said and who can speak and who must listen. Discourses shape how we operate in the world as human agents, construct consciousness, and what we consider true (Kincheloe, 2005).

Discrimination   A biased decision based on a prejudice against an individual group characterized by race, class, sexual orientation, age, disability, and so on (Adams, Bell, & Griffin, 2007).

Epistemology   A branch of philosophy that studies knowledge and its production (Kincheloe, 2005).

Ethnicity   A quality assigned to a specific group of people historically connected by a common national origin or language. Ethnic classification is used for identification rather than differentiation (Adams et al., 2007).

Ethnocentrism   A practice of unconsciously or consciously privileging a certain ethnic group over others. This involves judging other groups by the values of one's own group (J. Q. Adams, 2003).

Gender   The *psychological* orientation one has, typically based on our *biological* or birth sex (physical, hormonal, and genetic characteristics, though some are born *intersexed*, with some combination of male and female biological sex characteristics). However, for some people gender identity (how we identify ourselves) is incongruent with the sex they are assigned at birth. The spectrum of identities, then, is much broader than the woman-man binary and some people use terms like *genderqueer* or *transgender* to self-identify. *Gender roles* refer to the socially constructed behavioral and psychological characteristics expected of women and men. *Gender expression* challenges the gender binary (men and women) by disentangling gender from biological sex and provides a spectrum of possibilities for behavioral and psychological performance (Adams et al., 2007).

Hegemony   The process of moral and intellectual influence through which dominated or subordinate classes of people consent to their own domination, as opposed to being simply forced or coerced into accepting inferior positions. Hegemony controls the way new ideas are rejected or become naturalized in a process that subtly alters notions of common sense in a given society. Hegemony results in the empowerment of certain cultural beliefs, values, and practices to the submersion and partial exclusion of others (Adams et al., 2007).

Heterosexism   Individual, institutional, and societal-cultural beliefs and practices based on the belief that heterosexuality is the only normal and acceptable sexual orientation (Adams et al., 2007).

Homophobia   Aversion to or disapproval of physical intimacy and sexual expression between individuals of the same perceived sex; this aversion may range from mild to intense (Adams et al., 2007).

Internalized oppression   The "internalizing" or believing, on the part of a target group, the lies and misinformation that the agent group disseminates. It is expressed in behavior and interactions between individual members of the target group who repeat the content of the lies or misinformation. Internalized oppression is always an involuntary reaction to the experience of oppression on the part of the target group (Adams et al., 2007).

Institutional racism   The systematic use of economic and political power in institutions (such as schools) that leads to detrimental policies and practices. These policies and practices have a harmful effect on groups that share a particular identity (whether racial, ethnic, gender, or other). The major difference between individual and institutional discrimination is the wielding of power, because it is primarily through the power of the people who control institutions such as schools that oppressive policies and practices are reinforced and legitimated (J. Q. Adams, 2003).

Instrumental rationality   A dimension of positivist epistemology considered by critical theorists to be one of the most oppressive features of contemporary society. Critical theorists claim that instrumental or technical rationality is more interested in method and efficiency than in purpose. It limits questions to "how to," instead of "why should" (Kincheloe, 2005).

Marginality   The dilemma of individuals who are trapped between the macrocultures they can't fully assimilate into and their own indigenous culture, which they are no longer accepted in (J. Q. Adams, 2003).

Master narratives   Narratives are stories told from a personal point of view where identity is revealed and characters are cast. Master narratives, also known as "grand narratives," are the underlying stories that not only explain

(continued)

(continued)

but legitimize certain perspectives and knowledge. In the context of social relations, these myths function to legitimatize existing power relations, customs, and practices (J. Q. Adams, 2003).

Multiculturalism The practice of acknowledging and respecting the various cultures, religions, races, ethnicities, attitudes, and opinions within an environment (J. Q. Adams, 2003).

Objectivism The epistemological belief that disinterested knowledge can be produced about any phenomenon simply by following the scientific method (Kincheloe, 2005).

Oppression The systematic, institutionalized, pervasive, and routine mistreatment of individuals on the basis of their membership in groups that are disadvantaged by the imbalances in social power in society. Oppression must have societal or institutional power and prejudice (power + prejudice = "ism") (Adams et al., 2007).

Positionality The shifting ways individuals are located within broader societal structures of political, cultural, and economic domination, and of equality. Thus, gender, race, culture, sexual orientation, and social class, for example, are historically based, representing evolving sets of relational dynamics, rather than fixed identities (J. Q. Adams, 2003).

Positivism An epistemological position that values objective scientific knowledge produced in rigorous adherence to the scientific method. It identifies knowledge as worthwhile to the extent that it describes objective data that reflect the world (Kincheloe, 2005).

Praxis The process of connecting reflection with action in the pursuit of knowledge and social change (J. Q. Adams, 2003).

Prejudice Exerting bias and bigotry based on uniform stereotypes (Adams et al., 2007).

Privilege Unearned rights, benefits, immunity, and favors that are bestowed on individuals and groups solely on the basis of their race, culture, religion, gender, sexual orientation, physical ability, or other key characteristic (Adams et al., 2007).

Propriospect The sum total of an individual's experiences that functions as a sort of filter that either facilitates or inhibits communication toward accomplishing many purposes. (J. Q. Adams, 2003).

Race   An invalid paradigm developed to justify the different treatment accorded to different people through attempts to divide human groups according to physical characteristics (J. Q. Adams, 2003).

Racial and ethnic identity   An individual's awareness and experience of being a member of a racial and ethnic group; the racial, ethnic categories that an individual chooses to describe himself or herself based on such factors as biological heritage, physical appearance, cultural affiliation, socialization, or personal experience (Adams et al., 2007).

Racism   The systematic subordination of members of targeted racial groups who have relatively little social power in the United States (blacks, Latinos and Latinas, Native Americans, and Asians) by members of the agent racial group who have relatively more social power (whites). This subordination is supported by the actions of individuals, cultural norms and values, and the institutional structures and practices of society. While race as a concept is completely socially constructed, racism is real and has material consequences (Adams et al., 2007).

Sexism   The cultural, institutional, and individual set of beliefs and practices that privilege men, subordinate women, and denigrate values and practices associated with women (Adams et al., 2007).

Sexual orientation   One's predominant sexual and romantic attractions toward persons of the same sex (lesbian or gay), another sex (heterosexual), or any sex (bisexual) (Adams et al., 2007).

Social justice   Connotes both a process and a goal. The goal is full and equal participation of all groups in a society that is mutually shaped to meet their needs. The vision of such a society promotes (a) equitable distribution of resources, (b) physical and psychological safety and security, (c) self-determination and independent agency, and (d) a sense of self and responsibility to society as a whole. The vision of a socially just process includes practices and procedures that are democratic and participatory, inclusive and affirming of human capacities for working collaboratively to create change (Adams et al., 2007).

Target group   A group of people who are systemically conditioned to become victims of oppression (Reason et al., 2005).

(continued)

(continued)

References

Adams, J. Q. (Contributing Ed.). (2003). In J. W. Collins III & N. P. O'Brien, *The Greenwood dictionary of education.* Westport, CT: Greenwood Press.

Adams, M., Bell, L. A., & Griffin, P. (2007). *Teaching for diversity and social justice: A sourcebook.* New York: Routledge.

Kincheloe, J. L. (2005). *Critical constructivism primer.* New York: Peter Lang.

Reason, R., Broido, E., Davis, T., & Evans, N. (2005). *Developing social justice allies.* New Directions for Student Services, No. 110. San Francisco: Jossey-Bass.

Some of these concepts, we hope, are familiar, while others may be completely new. It is important to carefully listen to the nuances of the terms defined in Exhibit 2.1, especially those you believe you understand based on past interpretation. After deeper reflection, we have often found that our understanding of a term may be quite different from earlier conceptions. For example, the term *hegemony* is complex and multifaceted, and the more we reflect upon and practice using the meanings associated with it, the more we have used it as one lens that helps make sense of some phenomenon. Reading Noam Chomsky's (2003) definition of the term compared to Antonio Gramsci's (2000) original reflections can help provide a more integrated, differentiated comprehension, but will still require being open to new knowledge. Chomsky, for example, focuses in on hegemony's domination of the many by a few, particularly in the context of military dominance exerted by the United States. Gramsci elucidates an intricate theory of hegemony that describes the spontaneous consent given by most citizens to policies and practices designed by those in control of production through a sort of prestige hierarchy, where people acquiesce when doing so is not in their best interests.

While grasping the terms outlined here and maintaining an ability to (re)negotiate their meanings as new filters of knowledge are developed is important, it is not sufficient for constructing a framework for understanding or practicing social justice in higher education. To make meaning of social justice in higher education, we must also comprehend the complexities of individual identity development and institutional systems of oppression.

Social Construction of Identities: Positionality, Dominance, and Subordination

In the United States, we are socialized to believe in the sanctity of individual rights and the values of individualism. This is an example of a "master narrative," as described in Exhibit 2.1. One of the constructed stories perpetuated by this ideology is that individual identity represents the autonomous, independent construction of self. Contesting this myth is the wealth of evidence that suggests identities are critically influenced by history, context, traditions, and larger cultural narratives (Abes, Jones, & McEwen, 2007; D'Augelli, 1994; Davis, 2002; Davis, Thomas, & Sewalish, 2006; Josselson, 1996; Torres, Jones, & Renn, 2009; Vygotsky, 1978). Josselson (1996), for example, maintains that "identity is not just a private, individual matter [but] a complex negotiation between person and society" (p. 31). The construction of identity happens, therefore, as people negotiate cultural contexts, interact with other people, and absorb the cultural messages that surround them.

Understanding identity as socially constructed interrupts the notion that individual hard work and character are the only forces at play in determining who succeeds and who doesn't, and who has access to vital resources and who has hurdles in the pursuit of life, liberty, and happiness. In what ways do you see the myth of meritocracy reinforced in the culture today? The history described in Chapter Three clearly illustrates how policies and practices have inhibited such pursuits for people on the basis of ethnicity, sex, religion, class, and sexual orientation. Once we stop ignoring the impact of our cultural surroundings and the salience that race, class, and social categories have on our sense of self, we see that people can be dominant or subordinated on the basis of group status. Those who hold dominant status in a group, like men in a patriarchy, are sometimes referred to as agents or advantaged (Adams, Bell, & Griffin, 2007). Those who are subordinated or marginalized are sometimes identified as targets. These terms describe social locations of people based on their membership in a group or category of people who are either privileged or disadvantaged by systems of oppression. In addition, it is critical to be conscious of historical context. For example, a gay male will likely have considerably different identity experiences in 1940 compared to 2012, in small-town Alabama compared to downtown San Francisco, and so on. These contexts are, furthermore, experienced differently depending on one's internalized sense of self at the time and place. While it is beyond the purview of this book, there are numerous models of identity that describe the processes, statuses, or stages of people's development along various dimensions of identity (Abes, Jones, & McEwen, 2007; Cass, 1979; Cross, 1995; D'Augelli, 1994; Ferdman & Gallegos, 2001; Helms, 1990; Horse, 2001; Josselson, 1996; Kim, 2001; Marcia, 2002; Parks, 2005; Phinney, 1993; Wijeyesinghe, 2001).

An interesting and potentially sensitizing exercise we encourage you to perform to better understand this identity aspect of our conceptual framework is offered in Table 2.1. This short survey will help you better understand who you are not just in terms of labels but with regard to the relative *position* you hold in society and the advantages and disadvantages you experience. The goal is not to provoke guilt or embarrassment if you are advantaged, nor anger or overwhelming powerlessness if you are disadvantaged; after all, most of the statuses are not a result of personal choice, though there is potent institutional salience to them. Rather, the exercise should help you become more conscious about what is given freely to you

Table 2.1. **Identifying Advantages and Disadvantages of Your Identities**

Identity Category	Your Personal Identification	What Benefits Are Afforded?	What Challenges Are Encountered?
Gender			
Social class			
Cultural background			
Physical stature (height and weight)			
Skin color			
Ethnicity			
Educational background			
Sexual orientation			
Age			
Disability status			
Language(s) spoken			
Other category:			

and denied to others through systems of oppression. Privilege is used in the context of social justice as a way of describing unearned rights, benefits, and immunities granted to some based solely on their ethnicity, religion, gender, sexual orientation, physical ability, or other key characteristic. Our experience is that our own privilege is often invisible and sometimes difficult to identify. For example, most "white" people do not think of themselves in terms of race, and most men do not think of themselves in terms of gender. This "invisibility" is another defining characteristic of privilege that makes understanding and empathizing with someone who does not have related advantages difficult. Moreover, there are obvious incentives for keeping privileges hidden or even denying their existence. Invisibility maintains the status quo or any systematic act that unfairly distributes resources.

In addition to the exercise in Table 2.1, we invite you to consider the following questions to illuminate how our lives may be different from others based on our privileges. How might the experience of a male-identified student be different from a female-identified student walking home from the library at 1 a.m., applying for a part-time job as a nurse, or teaching in front of a class composed entirely of the opposite sex? How might a heterosexual person's experience differ from the experience of someone who is gay when expressing affection in public, introducing a partner to their family, or seeking couples counseling? Of course, we cannot really know how someone representing diverse identities will experience various situations without asking the person directly. The purpose here is not to define an experience, but to build empathy for life events that may never be ours. An important distinction here is the difference between empathy and sympathy. We should aim to listen for someone's lived experience so that we can understand and be with them (empathy), as opposed to feeling bad for them or pitying them (sympathy). The survey can also illuminate how our identities are connected through institutional salience and offers an opportunity for both the advantaged and disadvantaged to see that liberation requires working together to interrogate systematic oppression that keeps the former ignorant and the latter subjugated. In addition, we can use the survey to more intentionally consider people's position to better understand them and their relationship to us.

The ways in which we are "positioned" in society affects our encounters within it and our subsequent identity development. Individuals interested in promoting social justice in higher education will need to be conscious of their own position and the fact that others will be socially located in a different manner. According to Dolby (2000), "instead of probing what identities are and how they structure experience (or what identities a person has), the critical questions revolve around how 'difference is produced in a particular situation, how it is explained, circulated, and reproduced, and how 'difference' as a construct interfaces with various structures of power" (p. 901). In setting a central developmental task of students in higher education, Dolby challenges us to situate identity within the broad realities of environmental press and the salient influences of power and systematic oppression. Doing so liberates educators from the myth of the separate-unfolding-self, by giving appropriate attention to social influence. Sleeter and Grant (1994) further contend that social justice education should encourage students to reflect on their oppressed or privileged standing in order to judiciously understand the world around them. Similarly, in a study of students' comprehension of social justice concepts, Chizhik and Chizhik (2002) recommend that "educators of social justice need to spend quality time dissecting the construct of privilege" (p. 806). An important caution to keep in mind, however, is that given the multiple dimensions of identity, virtually no one is totally subordinated or completely privileged.

Identity Intersections: Border Crossing for Empathy

Several scholars provide theoretical bases for making meaning of multiple dimensions of identity and their complex intersectionalities (Crenshaw, 1989, 1991; Jones & McEwen, 2000; McCall, 2005; Shields, 2008). A focus on intersections of identity became necessary as academic feminists began illuminating the institutional subordination of women in U.S. society. According to Shields (2008), the question arose, "Which women's experience?" (p. 302). Crenshaw (1989) and others provided a critique that challenged the middle-class, highly educated, European-descent focus of the women's movement at the time to become inclusive of women with other social identities, especially non-European race or ethnicity. More recently, Dill and Zambrana (2009) offered the following description of intersectionality as

Characterized by the following four theoretical interventions: (1) Placing the lived experiences and struggles of people of color and other marginalized groups as a starting point for the development of theory; (2) exploring the complexities not only of individual identities but also group identity, recognizing that variations within groups are often ignored and essentialized; (3) unveiling the ways interconnected domains of power organize and structure inequality and oppression; and (4) promoting social justice and social change by linking research and practice to create a holistic approach to the eradication of disparities and to changing social and higher education institutions [p. 5].

Defining intersectionality in this manner is important for several reasons. First, it provides a lens through which a whole range of social identities and the related connections to privilege and subordination can be seen. The vast majority of people are not entirely privileged or entirely subordinated; rather, they have dimensions of identity that may be targeted for oppression and dimensions that may be advantaged. In Kaufman's (1999) articulation of contradictory experiences of power, for example, he says that "the social power of a poor man is different than a rich one, a working class black man from a working class white man, a gay man from a bisexual man from a straight man, a Jewish man in Ethiopia from a Jewish man in Israel, a teenage boy from an adult" (p. 68). In other words, rather than essentializing identity or its correlations to power and oppression, intersectionality provides a conceptual framework for comprehending the complex realities of the multidimensional, historically situated, contextually influenced nature of lived experience.

A second reason that Dill and Zambrana's (2009) definition of intersectionality as both theory and intervention is important is that it provides a framework for bringing everyone into the playing field of social justice. We have found that too often those with agent identities (particularly those who are "white," male, Christian, heterosexual, or upper class) are left out of or at least feel marginalized by discussions of multiculturalism, diversity, or social justice. One of the central reasons for this is that we tend to conflate the personal with the institutional. As a result, those with agent identities feel helpless to change who they are, rather than realizing that it's systematic oppression that needs to be challenged. Thus, discussions about social justice are necessarily inclusive of everyone: some are privileged and some subordinated by institutional oppression. While those targeted for oppression (or more accurately, those with dimensions of identity that are subordinated) are generally more conscious of institutional oppression and are certainly more likely to suffer the material and psychological consequences of those systems, they also have identity dimensions that can sensitize them to the experience of privilege and agency. Similarly, those advantaged by oppression have windows to empathy based on identity dimensions that may be disadvantaged. Empathy, or the ability to sense and understand what someone else is experiencing, appears to be a significant factor in social justice education. It stands to reason that unless we can empathize with another person's experience of either institutional advantages or disadvantages, we will be ineffective in engaging them in discussions about systematic oppression. Those unable to feel or think about another person's difficulties will not see the need for change, at best. Research, in fact, suggests that antisocial, prejudicial, and criminal dispositions are tightly correlated with a reduced ability to appreciate the experiences of others (Decety & Jackson, 2004; Gutsell & Inzlicht, 2010). Fortunately, helping individuals develop an understanding of their own experiences of privilege and oppression offers possibilities for becoming sensitized to how another person might feel or think.

Even if someone exists who has only privileged identities, there are disadvantages to the advantages. Kelly's (2008) study of young white men illustrated not only how men negotiated their privileges differently, but also how some became conscious of the steep price they paid for colluding with systems of domination. One participant, for example, described the simultaneous experiences he had of dehumanizing acquiescence to rigid roles and the benefits of being of the dominant race and sex. Hardiman and Jackson (2007) described such individuals as being "trapped by the system of social oppression that benefits them, and are confined to the roles and prescribed behavior for their group" (p. 37). Similarly, Freire (2000) suggested that the acts of the oppressor lead him or her to dehumanizing, necrophilic existence. Centrally, the invisibility of privilege and oppression has important, but similarly invisible costs for agents. Another way of framing these "disadvantages for those who are advantaged by systematic oppression" is that there are important ontological and other incentives to join in an active implementation of social justice. What is clear from this section is that our efforts toward promoting social justice need to focus less on individual identities and more on the systems that enforce privilege and oppression, less on essentialist notions of identity politics and more on multiple dimensions of identity where everyone has cards to play—and more on the very real costs of unconsciously participating as an agent in domination.

Systems of Power, Oppression, and Structural Inequality

If you identified few disadvantages in Table 2.1 or if your identity dimensions are predominantly privileged, the concept of oppression may seem somewhat abstract and possibly even untenable. In fact, the master narrative described earlier in which individualism is valorized leads to skepticism about the influence of anything outside of the individual. The narrative is literarily canonized by Horatio Alger's mythical stories, which implied that any poor boy with patience and an unwavering commitment to hard work can overcome nearly anything to become a dazzling success. In addition, even those who are targeted for oppression are exposed to these same fundamental assumptions associated with individualism. Hosting such beliefs can lead to the internalized oppression described in Exhibit 2.1 and internalized superiority in those who are agents. For example, a study by Bertrand and Mullainathan (2004) found that people with "black-sounding names" were 50 percent less likely to be invited for an interview than those with "white-sounding names." Someone hosting internalized oppression might believe that he or she is undeserving of the interview, as opposed to locating the problem in the institutionalized forces of racism. Similarly, those with white-sounding names might begin to believe that they are being interviewed because of their skills only, as the privilege described by Bertrand and Mullainathan remains invisible to those who receive it. Yamato (2004) further clarified this phenomenon when she wrote that being a black woman "influences the way I see or don't see myself, limits what I expect of myself or others like me. It results in my acceptance of mistreatment, leads me to believe that being treated with less than absolute respect, at least this once, is to be expected" (p. 66). Franz Fanon (2008), in his landmark book *Black Skin, White Masks*, powerfully described the devastating psychological effects of colonialism on the colonized. Whether generally targeted or advantaged by oppression, we have all been inundated by messages in the United States that suggest that individuals receive the treatment they have earned and any theories of oppression that focus on systems, institutions, or external environments are suspect at best.

This point is important because oppression is not the sum of attitudes and behaviors of individuals acting independently. Oppression, rather, is the structural, systemic, institutionalized, pervasive, and routine mistreatment of individuals on the basis of their membership in various groups who are disadvantaged by the imbalances in social power in society. Moreover, oppression "pervades social institutions and practices, and it shapes the very nature of our social world" (Heldke & O'Connor, 2004, p. 1). The central conceptual basis for social justice education is rooted in theories of oppression. As such, social justice is the antithesis of oppression or the liberation from it. The central features of oppression will be discussed throughout the rest of this chapter.

Historically, oppression has served to describe overt brutality like the treatment of black Africans during apartheid in South Africa or the treatment of Jews by Nazi Germany. The meaning of oppression in this book, on the other hand, proposes that while these are accurate portrayals of oppression, the injustices people typically suffer today come not from tyrannical dictatorships, but from "everyday practices of a well-intentioned liberal society" (Young, 2004, p. 38). In this way, oppression is structurally embedded in unquestioned habits, norms, and the kind of commonsense knowledge that causes people to become blinded to the enculturation they receive. Another name for this process of influence where we learn to earnestly embrace a system of beliefs and practices that essentially harm us, while working to uphold the interests of others who have power over us, is *hegemony*. According to Brookfield (2005), "ideology becomes hegemony when the dominant ideas are learned and lived in everyday decisions and judgments and when these ideas (reinforced by the mass media images and messages) pervade the whole existence" (p. 94). One needs only to view a few hours of prime-time television and included commercials to see, for example, how uniformly restrictive sex roles are portrayed and reinforced as normal. The sex role ideology becomes so ingrained and reinforced by other socializing agents that we not only consent to it willingly, we begin to believe that anyone who acts outside of these roles is weird or wrong.

Another important feature of oppression, in addition to its deeply embedded, pervasive inconspicuousness, is its location in systems, not necessarily in people. While people are influenced by systems and generally follow their rules, according to Young (2004), "the systemic character of oppression implies that an oppressed group need not have a correlate oppressing group" (p. 39). Thus, oppression is not necessarily embodied by a conscious oppressor, but alternatively embedded in the kinds of systems, policies, and practices that explain the racist findings Bertrand and Mullainathan (2004) described earlier. Foucault (1980) similarly said that we need to analyze the exercise of power not in the traditional notions of oppressor-oppressed, but instead in the humane practices of education, bureaucracies, private production and distribution of goods, health care, and the like.

Although we tend to think of ethnicity, class, sexual orientation, and other identity dimensions as preferences, styles, cultural practices, or ways of being, we need to widen our view to include the additional dimension that these aspects of self are socially situated within power hierarchies. There are "substantial material and nonmaterial resources—such as wealth, income, or access to health care and education that are at stake" (Weber, 1998, p. 18). Central to the differentiation we make between males and females, gays and heterosexuals, and other identity dimensions is the exploitation of one group for the purposes of acquiring greater resources. A historical example of this is the African slave trade, where racist ideologies were constructed in order to legitimize commercial interests of the ruling class. Takaki (1993) describes how the indentured servant system of cheap labor in the seventeenth century gave way to enslavement of Africans in part because it became easier to distinguish who was a slave through physical features. In addition, a propaganda campaign based on those same features ensued that dehumanized Africans, providing a rationale for their barbaric treatment. The resulting cheap labor served the colonial elite, from an economic standpoint, quite well. Contemporary evidence of this is the disproportionate gender distribution in the current U.S. Congress, where in the House of Representatives there are 355 men and 78 women, and in the Senate only 20 women of 100 total senators. Readers should also look to see how ethnicity, religion, and other salient identity groups are represented in federal and state decision-making bodies. Since systematic power relationships exist in a manner that advantages some and disadvantages others, social justice education, scholarship, and practice need to focus not only on how targets are subordinated, but also how agents are advantaged.

In addition to oppression being systemic, pervasive, restrictive, and hierarchical, it is complicated by the identity dimensions and intersections described in the previous section. Since most of us have both dominant and subordinate identity dimensions, individuals cannot be reduced to their membership in any one racial, gender, religious, sexual, socioeconomic, or other group. Moreover, these identity dimensions are not immutable or permanent characteristics, but are dynamically in flux depending on context, historical location, and the audience in front of whom the actors are performing. Instead, identities are coconstructions between self and environment "that often give us power and option in some arenas while restricting our opportunities in others" (Weber, 1998, p. 21). As such, oppressions do not add up like math, so that having three targeted dimensions is more oppressed than having two. Arguments about one form of oppression being worse than another cannot be based on one dimension of identity. Moreover, those arguing for a "hierarchy of oppression" often do so by focusing horizontally at other groups who are oppressed, leaving vertical oppression and those who are privileged completely uninterrogated. Horizontal oppression refers to target group members enforcing subordinate status on their own group or another targeted group. An example of this is a woman opposing equal rights or a Latino father telling his lighter-skinned daughter she is more beautiful than her darker-skinned sister. Vertical oppression exists when agents subordinate targets, as when white men pass laws that restrict women or people of color. Privilege and subordination, as we've been arguing throughout this chapter, are historically influenced and contextually situated. They are also dynamic. The complexities described here illustrate how important it is to be conscious of ways that we are positioned and how those around us benefit or are disadvantaged in particular situations. Such awareness is required for us to work with different groups, developing the kind of empathy and abilities to achieve a more equitable distribution of social, cultural, and economic resources.

Until now we have treated oppression as if it played out the same way for every group of people. We believe, however, that while the dynamics of oppression are similar for various targeted groups, there are multiple manifestations of it. Like Adams, Bell, and Griffin (2007), we believe that there is important explanatory and political value in describing the particular histories and unique ways in which expressions of oppression like racism, sexism, heterosexism, classism, ableism, ageism, and religious subjugation play out in this culture. We encourage readers not only to consider how different historical and social contingencies affect one form of oppression versus another, but to read the histories outlined by Takaki (1993) or Zinn (2005). Doing so will equip educators with the ability to see how different histories shape contemporary identities, as well as insight into the types of appropriate policies, practices, and political action necessary to confront the various manifestations of oppression. Certainly experiences of oppression can be similar or dramatically different. The range of experiences requires that educators have a strong sense of unique histories, combined with the knowledge to avoid simplistic binary terms and essentialized identity dimensions, and the ability to empathetically ask questions and listen to different voices. Like Young (2004) and Adams, Bell, and Griffin (2007), we think that eradicating oppression ultimately requires addressing all of its forms and that diverse groups of people, both targeted and advantaged, offer the best chance to effectively promote social justice.

Wealth, Power, and Access: How Are We Doing?

At the beginning of this chapter we asked the question, "If equal liberty, equal justice, and equal rights are fundamental to the U.S. democracy, as suggested by our founding fathers and reinforced by leaders since, how would one measure whether or not our actions are congruent with our aims?" One measure is to look at the material outcomes most valued by this society and see if they are equitably distributed. So how are we doing? From a distribution-of-resources perspective, the wealth gap in the United States is the greatest it has been since just before the Great Depression in the 1930s. According to the 2010 census, there are nearly 309,000,000 people in the United States; the total wealth of the top 400 individuals is more than the bottom 185,400,000 combined. As of 2007, the top 1 percent of households (the upper class) owned 34.6 percent of all privately held wealth, and the next 19 percent (the managerial, professional, and small-business stratum) had 50.5 percent, which means that just 20 percent of the people owned a remarkable 85 percent, leaving only 15 percent of the wealth for the bottom 80 percent (wage and salary workers). In addition, the top 1 percent of the population control 40 percent of the wealth. The top 1 percent saw their incomes rise 275 percent between 1979 and 2007 (Wolff, 2010).

We already outlined the gender disparity in the 113th Congress in which men are disproportionately represented, but what about ethnic composition? Table 2.2 illustrates that 82 percent of Congress is "white" and that there is only one "black" senator. In addition, only 5 percent of the Senate is nonwhite. It's a little more than ironic that a government supposedly "by the people, for the people" is not representative of the people. There are also significant correlations with ethnicity and poverty, ethnicity

Table 2.2.   Racial Composition of the 113th Congress

	U.S. House	U.S. Senate
White	355	95
Black	40	1
Latino	28	3
Asian and Pacific Islander	9	1
American Indian	1	0

Source: Congress.org, January 2013.

and educational attainment, and other factors that portray a system with wide gaps between equal opportunities promised and equal justice realized. While social justice actions have occasionally reduced the distance in some gaps, like the Civil Rights policies described in Chapter Three, the statistics we offer here illustrate that we are far from fulfilling our constitutional promises.

There are in fact reasons to believe that not only are these gaps being ignored, but that policies offering hope for social justice in higher education are being scaled back. During the last few years when Wall Street banks were being bailed out, scholarship programs for underrepresented students like the McNair Scholarship program were being dismantled. The U.S. Department of Education proposed cutting funding by $10 million in the summer of 2012, thereby reducing the number of schools offering scholarships by 20 to 30 percent. Colleges have also moved away from economic need to merit aid. Affirmative action programs that have demonstrably reduced inequality in educational opportunity are under assault. In addition, as much as higher education has been called the great equalizer, this no longer seems to be true. A study by Stanford University shows that the gap in standardized-test scores between low-income and high-income students has widened about 40 percent since the 1960s (Reardon, 2011). A study from the University of Michigan similarly found that the disparity in college-completion rates between rich and poor students has grown by about 50 percent since the 1980s (Bailey & Dynarski, 2011). In addition, low-income and minority students are concentrated in community colleges, which spent an average of $12,957 per full-time-equivalent student in 2009, while higher-income and white students are disproportionately educated at private four-year research institutions, which spent an average of $66,744 per student (Kahlenberg, 2012b). The need for continued diligence to promote social justice is clear. Abraham Lincoln, for example, believed equality should be something "constantly looked to, constantly labored for, and even though never perfectly attained, constantly approximated, and thereby constantly spreading and deepening its influence, and augmenting the happiness and value of life to all people of all colors everywhere" (Basler, 1953, p. 407). He challenged America to strive toward the perfection of equality at all times. We argue that while equality is a valid outcome, equity is more appropriate given human differences and differential histories.

Conclusion

Social justice is described in this chapter as essentially bridging the gap between mission statement and action. Its successful implementation requires recognition that people and their histories are different, and equity demands fair treatment where those differences are not ignored. To bridge these differences, we believe that action needs to be guided by a clear conceptual vision. Our conceptual framework for social justice is grounded in constructivist assumptions that people and institutions create policies, practices, and procedures that advantage some and disadvantage others. As a result, power, wealth, and other resources are disproportionately distributed, and social justice, as described in our founding documents, requires us to respond with equity and fairness. The wide diversity of people, their multiple dimensions of identity, and complex intersectionalities combined with systematic oppression deeply embedded in the fabric of our institutions add to an intricate phenomenon that is easy to misunderstand. Further complicating the illumination of such a phenomenon are the master narratives, uninterrogated commonsense knowledge, and hegemonies described throughout this chapter.

To counter this multifaceted matrix, in this chapter we offer conceptual tools, including theories of identity and oppression, along with terminology connected to these frameworks in order for readers to develop their own personalized praxis. We also hope this chapter helps clarify why some will resist a social justice framework.

After all, if social justice is simply bridging the gap between what we say as a country and what we do, why would someone resist such a framework? You should now have some answers. We've also seen how systematic oppression has material and psychological implications for both those targeted for oppression and those advantaged by it. Educators wanting to address these issues need to familiarize themselves with not only the framework offered here, but the unique histories and social contingencies experienced by their students.

While we will continue to outline hurdles to social justice in the following chapters, we will also outline key strategies that we believe are necessary to once again begin addressing the gaps in our espoused mission—described in the two quotes that opened this chapter—and enacted reality. Gaining a working knowledge of empathy, organizational theory, media literacy, critical pedagogy, and other key concepts will be essential for meeting contemporary challenges with effective praxis—the kind of praxis described by Freire and enacted by those like Dr. Martin Luther King Jr., Jane Addams, W.E.B. DuBois, Charlotte Perkins Gilman, Cesar Chavez, Saul Alinsky, Howard Zinn, and Eleanor Roosevelt, who have made significant lasting social change toward justice. Freireian pedagogy and praxis will be described in Chapters Five and Eight, but for now we mean consciously employing the toolkit just described in ways that develop agency rather than dependence, encourage interrogation rather than complacency, and move us toward liberation rather than replication. This chapter illustrated the sort of tools one has to develop, but only implied the kind of nuanced practice one has to cultivate in order to accomplish what these great leaders have achieved. Taking these definitions and concepts into practice is the aim of the rest of this book.

3

From Wealthy White Landowners to Affirmative Action to Proposition 209 to *Grutter v. Bollinger*

A Short History of Social Justice and Injustice in Higher Education

To be hopeful in bad times is not just foolishly romantic. It is based on the fact that human history is a history not only of cruelty but also of compassion, sacrifice, courage, kindness. What we choose to emphasize in this complex history will determine our lives. If we see only the worst, it destroys our capacity to do something. If we remember those times and places—and there are so many—where people have behaved magnificently, this gives us the energy to act, and at least the possibility of sending this spinning top of a world in a different direction. And if we do act, in however small a way, we don't have to wait for some grand utopian future. The future is an infinite succession of presents, and to live now as we think human beings should live, in defiance of all that is bad around us, is itself a marvelous victory.

—Howard Zinn (2004)

So far we've defined social justice in terms of bridging the gap between what our society aspires to and what we actually do. Many, however, are unaware of the existence of a gap or what creates it. Those with privilege, as described in Chapter Two, do not generally encounter the barriers that those who are targeted for oppression must negotiate. The gap, in other words, routinely remains invisible. Further hiding the roots of contemporary disparities is the invisibility of history. This chapter will illuminate some important events in history related to social justice in higher education that too often are either left out of history books or overshadowed by larger grand narratives.

The history of social justice in U.S. higher education mirrors the broader cultural history of America: the story is full of narrow ethnocentrism, exclusionary policies and practices, and other forms of oppression, as well as courageous responses that have opened the doors for people to build the futures they desire. Moreover, it is impossible to understand social justice in higher education outside of the contours of American culture and American history. Contemporary issues related to equity, access, multiculturalism, and affirmative action were not uprooted and planted in the twenty-first century, but have evolved from efforts to address injustice since the founding of this great country. Failing to understand history means failing to understand contemporary efforts to move our society toward the kind of democracy promised in our U.S. Constitution. History, furthermore, illustrates as much about the present and future as the past. According to Levstik and Barton (2000), "when we identify with groups in history, we stake our identities in the present; when we look at where the world has been, we hope we will understand where it is going; when we judge the decisions of the past, we promise to make better ones next time" (p. 2). In order for history to fulfill such roles, however, we need a deep and inclusive exposure to it.

In this chapter we invite you to "do history" with us. One purpose of this book is to move beyond a passive, esoteric representation of social justice and invite readers to actively and critically engage, debate, and disagree with the ideas presented. Doing history, like doing social justice, is brought to life in active implementation, rather than only passive reflection. Implementation needs, however, to be guided by critical consciousness—of history, of one's position in relation to historical events, and of rigorous processes involved in analyzing the past within the present context. We may, for example, have different interpretations of the same historical event based on our identity positions related to sex, gender, ethnic heritage, spirituality, socioeconomic class, sexual orientation, and/or disability status. History, in other words, is a part of who we are. I (Davis) would think of myself and the world differently if my ancestors came to the United States in 2001, rather than coming to America from Italy in the early 1900s. My current experience is distinctive if my ancestors came to America seeking job opportunities, as opposed to seeking political asylum or being forced onto a ship to work as a slave in a foreign country. Refusing to empathize with how other people may experience the same events results in a failure to understand the past, much less engage in civil dialogue in the present. This is not a request for us all to get along, or even to agree, but to decide on some basic necessities of informed engagement.

Here we will trace the ambivalent history of social justice in higher education to situate the present text within this larger historical framework. We will consider how concepts like equity, access, diversity, multiculturalism, and affirmative action have shaped our imaginations about *whom* college is *for*. We will, in short, provide our perspective on the historical shifts that bring us to the contemporary need for a social justice framework capable of encompassing complexities like identity intersectionality, institutional power, and deep empathy for those with opposing views. If you are willing to "do history" with us, you will need to actively frame your own questions, gather additional data from reputable sources, organize and interpret facts, and share your findings with others participating in this human drama. Our goal is not to feed you passive history lessons, but to challenge you to discover for yourself what happened in history, what stories are left out of the public discourse, whose stories are told or ignored, and to what ends. It is important to cocreate learning partnerships where knowledge is constructed around and guided by accepted scholarly practices so that "truths" are not dogmatically given and accepted like many of the partial histories initially taught earlier in students' educational experience. In other words, challenging distorted and incomplete perspectives about history requires activating student reexamination of uncritically received knowledge, not replacing one dogma with another. This also means that one needs to be familiar with multiple and competing sources. There are many outstanding history texts that detail the lived experiences of those in the margins of the narrative generally told in this country (for example, Solomon, 1985; Takaki, 1993; Zinn, 2005). It is beyond the scope of this book to detail these histories; what follows instead is a succinct overview of themes related to social justice in higher education in the United States in order to provide context for the rest of the book.

Unequal Opportunity and Injustice for All but a Few

Colonial colleges allowed only white Christian males to matriculate, while women, African Americans, and nearly everyone else was denied participation by either statute or custom. Some colleges did admit Native Americans, but only to convert them to Christianity and force assimilation to the Euro-American customs, language, and dress (Carney, 1999). The nation's elite, upper-class white men were educated and disproportionately became leaders in late eighteenth-century and early nineteenth-century politics, industry, and government. It raises the question, "in what ways is the historical centering of white, wealthy, Christian men evident in today's educational, political, and commercial institutions, and does this past affect current economic, legal, and social capital landscapes?" Similarly, how does such a historically exclusive route for success inhibit opportunities today for those prevented from education, land ownership, and other central means to wealth creation?

According to Solomon (1985), young women were eventually admitted to higher education following a national demand for trained teachers during the 1830s. In addition, families began desiring new ways for young single women to contribute to their welfare. It became possible for single women to achieve financial independence and respectability within a rigid social structure by attending a normal school or female seminary that provided an education for employment as teachers. While "white" and Christian women were allowed some expanded opportunities in education, it would be nearly another century before they acquired the fundamental right to vote. Some may not know that the state of Mississippi did not ratify the nineteenth amendment until 1984, more than sixty years after the law passed nationally (Swain, Payne, & Spruill, 2010). Even when coeducational institutions opened their doors to women, they were not always happy with the results. Solomon (1985) describes, for example, that the percentage of women at the University of Chicago reached 52 percent in 1902, and they received a majority of the Phi Beta Kappa awards. The response from the university president at the time was to retreat from full coeducation into sex-segregated classes. If you didn't already know these facts, why is this the first time you have heard them? Is it important to know that these realities existed? What does it mean for you to know?

Federal legislation like the Morrill Act of 1862, the Hatch Act, and the Second Morrill Act of 1890 established federal interest and involvement in education by bringing federal funding and projects to both public colleges and the newly established land-grant campuses. Federal involvement also represented a step toward social justice by including African Americans in higher education. The Morrill Act of 1890 provided funding for African American education, which led to the creation of African American–serving colleges (now commonly referred to as Historically Black Colleges and Universities or HBCUs) in more than a dozen southern states. While this represented one step forward in terms of expanding our democracy's promise of treating all people with equity, guidelines were written that allowed state and local practices of racial segregation. This meant that southern black children attended public schools that received fewer resources per pupil than public schools attended by white children. Margo (1990), for example, clearly illustrates how racial inequality in school resources led to racial differences in educational outcomes like school attendance, literacy rates, and standardized test scores. Moreover, even "equal" schools were not enough to compensate for 250 years of slavery and denial of fundamental human rights (Fry, 2004).

As you developed an understanding of history, were you taught only partial truths through texts that memorialized blemish-free heroines and heroes, described stories of a unilaterally forward-moving democracy, and elicited romantic images of hard-fought liberties with clear distinctions between those who were right (us, Christians, whites, and so on) and those who were evil (them, non-Christians, nonwhites, and so on)? Or were you taught a more nuanced perspective like the more contextually accurate effect of legislation like the Morrill Act of 1890 that served both as a step toward realizing democratic values and resulted in a reification of racist segregation? If the former, why would your education consist of incomplete or inaccurate facts? Who or what is served by the (his)stories we received? According to James Loewen, author of *Lies My Teacher Told Me: Everything Your American History Text Got Wrong* (1995) and *Lies Across America: What Our Historic Sites Get Wrong* (1999), the history most of us were taught is full of distortions, omissions, and hyperbole.

African Americans were not the only ethnic group prevented from acquiring the educational benefits that led to prosperity and the "American Dream." Native Americans, Mexican Americans, Chinese Americans, Japanese Americans—essentially anyone who fell on the wrong side of the white versus nonwhite binary—were denied the status, privilege, opportunities, and constitutional protections accessible to whites on the assumption of inherited and immutable traits (Harris, 1993; Takaki, 1998; Zinn, 2005). An example of nonwhites' exclusion from basic civil rights even in the early part of the twentieth century is the Supreme Court's decisions regarding race and citizenship. Between 1878 and 1909, the courts heard twelve cases regarding naturalization of applicants from China, Japan, Burma, and Hawaii, as well as several multiracial individuals. In eleven of twelve cases, the individuals were denied citizenship on the basis of their failure to be "white," using the so-called scientific classifications (Mongolian, Negro, Caucasian, Indian, and Malay) or a "common knowledge" criterion the courts used to determine who was white and who was not (Foley, 2005). In 1923, Takao Ozawa, a Japanese businessman who was educated at the University of California–Berkeley and a resident of the United States for twenty-eight years, was denied citizenship on the grounds that although he had "white skin," he was not Caucasian and "whiteness" by itself did not guarantee one's "property right" afforded by our democracy (Haney Lopez, 1997). Just three months later, the Supreme Court ruled in *United States v. Thind* (1923) that Bhagat Singh Thind, though Caucasian, was not white. Whiteness, the court ruled, was essentially whatever they said it was. What do you think the racial composition of the Supreme Court was during this decision? An excellent documentary that traces our country's confusing, contradictory, and powerfully oppressive construction of race is *Race: The Power of an Illusion* (Adelman & Herbes-Sommers, 2003).

Jewish people have also met hurdles to equity within higher education, ranging from institutional anti-Semitism that denied Jews the opportunity to join historically Christian fraternities to turn-of-the-twentieth-century quota requirements that limited admission to both undergraduate institutions (Horowitz, 1987; Takaki, 1993) and medical schools (Halperin, 2001). While Muslims began to immigrate to the United States as early as about 1875, they represent a relatively new demographic on the American higher education scene. According to Ali and Bagheri (2005), "in the United States, Islam has tended to be a religion that has not been well understood, and the terrorist attacks of September 11, 2001, resulted in an increase in the marginalization and discrimination of Muslims" (p. 48). Today, some Christians believe that public education persecutes Christians. Carl Parnell (2008), for example, writes, "Public schools have become the major breeding ground in America for Christian persecution" (p. 1). Oppression is complicated, requiring those interested in social justice to ask questions like: Is there a difference in the kind of discrimination faced by Jews and Muslims in history and what some describe as persecution of Christians in the United States? Historically, how many institutions of higher education have provided faith-based space, financial support through student fees, and support services for the various religions? Which faiths receive the bulk of this support, and which ones have historically faced physical violence, threats, and vandalism?

An underlying issue related to social justice in higher education that too often is not discussed, and therefore remains invisible, is social and economic class. According to Perrucci and Wyson (2002), "Class in America is a taboo subject because of the national reluctance to examine how the class system in the United States operates on a day-to-day basis" (p. 4). During the first century and a half of U.S. history, higher education was disproportionately populated with wealthy upper-class individuals, as the financial benefits of a college education for lower- and middle-class families had to be weighed against wage-earning employment. For most, this meant the costs of education often outweighed its prospective financial benefits. This began to change following World War II, as one of the most generous and flexible financial aid programs in the history of this country was provided to veterans to attend postsecondary institutions. In 1947, the Truman Commission on Higher Education in a Democracy and the 1944 Servicemen's Readjustment Act (aka the GI Bill) enabled an unprecedented number of people to attend college.

But even this apparent opening of the doors to access for higher education was clouded with mixed results. Consider the following facts regarding World War II outlined by Takaki (1993):

- 33,000 Japanese Americans fought abroad, while many of their Japanese American relatives were gathered and housed in internment camps.

- 8,800 out of 60,000 Native Americans between the ages of twenty-one and forty-four were in the military (a higher percentage than the general population).

- Although Mexican Americans composed only one-tenth of the Los Angeles, California, population, they represented one-fifth of the casualties.

- Before the war in 1940, only 5,000 blacks were in the U.S. Army; by 1944, there were 700,000.

One might hypothesize, then, that individuals from these minority populations would disproportionately reap the benefits of their service. Evidence suggests the contrary. According to Katznelson (2005), "the way in which the law and its programs were organized and administered, and its ready accommodation to the larger discriminatory context within which it was embedded, produced practices that were more racially distinct and arguably more cruel than any other New Deal–era program. The performance of the GI Bill mocked the promise of fair treatment" (pp. 140–141). For example, the veteran's on-the-job training program in Georgia approved 246 programs for training by 1946; black veterans took part in only six (Onkst, 1998). Discrimination was not limited to the South, however, as statistics show that of the 9,000 students at the University of Pennsylvania in 1946 (which had the least restrictive admissions policy in the Ivy League), only 46 were black (Herbold, 1994–1995). Turner and Bound (2003) similarly found that following the GI Bill, the gap in educational attainment between blacks and whites actually widened, rather than closed.

The GI Bill qualifies as the most wide-ranging set of social benefits ever offered by the federal government, and it essentially created the middle class through helping veterans with funding for college, business ventures, job training, and home purchases. A report summarizing studies by the Bureau of the Census, the Southern Regional Council, the Urban League, and the American Veterans Committee concluded that it was "as though the GI Bill had been earmarked for white veterans only" (Bolte & Harris, 1947, p. 20). Exemplifying their point are the so-called "redlining" practices of the Federal Home Administration underwriters, who warned that the presence of even one or two nonwhite families in a given neighborhood could undermine real estate values. These government guidelines were readily accepted by private industry, to the extent that race became as much of a factor in real estate assessment as property condition. Redlining practices prevented families of color from obtaining and sustaining homes. Illustrating the dramatic impact of these policies, between 1934 and 1962 the federal government underwrote $120 billion in new housing—less than 2 percent of it went to nonwhites (Adelman & Herbes-Sommers, 2003). If your grandfather had returned from military service and was prevented from receiving a home mortgage due to racial preferences, how would you feel when someone claims that we live in a meritocracy where people receive what they deserve based on hard work?

Redlining also served to solidify ethnically segregated and impoverished school districts, which are reinforced today through the policy of property tax funding of public schools. Redlining was a double-edged sword, inhibiting access to home mortgages and distributing inequitable public school funding, which severely cut the chances for nonwhites to gain access to higher education.

While the GI Bill offered eligible nonwhites more opportunities than seemed possible at the turn of the nineteenth century, it was riddled with imperfections that reflected the institutional racism of the time. Post–World War II legislation like the GI Bill also gave energy to civil rights cases linked with educational access. The U.S. Supreme Court's ruling in *Brown v. Board of Education*

(1954), overturning a "separate but equal" segregation policy, led to an increase in the number of underrepresented ethnic minorities being admitted to white institutions. However, the impact of the decision was felt more in K–12 education than higher education, as only 17 percent of the predominantly white postsecondary institutions admitted African Americans by 1961 (Forest & Kinser, 2002). It wasn't until civil rights legislation such as the Higher Education Act (HEA) of 1965 and the 1972 amendments of the HEA, including Title III and Title IV, that established direct financial aid to underrepresented students and funding for student support services, known as TRIO programs, that enrollments began to move toward equitable representation. In summary, even legislation touted as progressive must be examined closely to understand its role in contemporary social justice issues regarding access to higher education.

While there has been slow and contentious historical growth in access to higher education based on gender, ethnicity, religion, and socioeconomic class, identity-based discrimination based on disability, sexual orientation, and age also exists. For example, before the Individuals with Disabilities Education Act of 1975, a majority of the then almost four million children with disabilities were denied meaningful participation in public education. A federal study, in fact, found "a majority of handicapped [sic] children in the United States were either totally excluded from schools or [were] sitting idly in regular classrooms awaiting the time when they were old enough to 'drop out'" (H. R. Rep. No. 94–332, 1975, p. 2). The history related to sexual orientation and higher education suggests a cycling of acceptance and condemnation. According to Gibson and Meem (2005), partnerships between women were generally accepted in the late nineteenth and early twentieth century to the extent that "they could be treated with the kind of openness and respect characteristic of married heterosexual couples" (p. 4). Such tolerance began to disappear in the 1920s, and by the 1960s students identifying as gay were often dismissed from universities or received disciplinary action (Dilley, 2002). Higher education has recently made strides toward lesbian, gay, bisexual, and trans-gendered (LGBT) inclusiveness through instituting gender-neutral housing and bathrooms, educational programming, and other ini-tiatives to create equity and justice. On the other hand, a 2010 multi-institutional climate study found that LGBT respondents experience significantly greater harassment and discrimination than their heterosexual counterparts, resulting in lower educational outcomes, low self-esteem, and compromised emotional, mental, and physical health (Rankin, Blumenfeld, Weber, & Frazer, 2010). Historical oppression regarding each of these identities is outlined quite clearly in numerous texts that we highly recommend, includ-ing *Teaching for Diversity and Social Justice* (Adams, Bell, & Griffin, 2007), *Oppression, Privilege, and Resistance: Theoretical Perspectives on Racism, Sexism, and Heterosexism* (Heldke & O'Connor, 2004), *Developing Social Justice Allies* (Reason, Broido, Davis & Evans, 2005), *Disability Services and Campus Dynamics* (Harbour & Madaus, 2011), and *Toward Acceptance: Sexual Orientation Issues on Campus* (Wall & Evans, 1999).

Present Effects of Past Discrimination

Even if we do not detail each identity-based history separately, it should by now be clear that these identity dimensions are not unrelated. Adams et al. (2007) illustrate how issues of class, for example, intersect with nearly every other form of oppression. They indicate that people living in poverty are more likely to be disabled, female, or a person of color. In fact, "white people are disproportionately wealthy and poor people are disproportionately black, Latino, and Native American" (Adams et al., 2007, p. 310). From this intersectional and overlapping perspective, seeking social justice for anyone representing any identity is not simply a matter of cultivating fairness for the widely diverse group of individuals who identify with that label, but rather an issue of creating policies and institutions "that are more just for everyone—that eschew all types of discrimination, invite investment and engagement, and offer opportunities for everyone to succeed" (Peltier Campbell, 2012). An important point of common cause among all people who have experienced oppression is highlighted here as an antidote to the identity politics of the past, where activists argued for a hierarchy of oppression where the focus was on in-group and out-group issues. In other words, identity-based politics that focus on simply one identity need to yield to more inclusive strategies that focus on systems of oppression that limit justice for all. Debates about who has it worse leave the *structures* of oppression uninterrogated.

Just as there is a relationship between wealth and identity characteristics, there is a clear connection between the historical oppression described in the preceding paragraphs and current wealth today. Any honest appraisal of wealth disparities among ethnic groups, for instance, cannot ignore historical realities like the middle-class creating FHA loans after World War II that left nonwhites behind. In fact, we argue that redlining, Supreme Court decisions to exclude nonwhites, and other policies, practices, and procedures in this country constitute "affirmative action" policies—but aimed to promote the interests of those in power and with privilege. In other words, we've described historical action that has affirmed white, Christian, able-bodied, heterosexual men and excluded others. In an ironic twist, what was considered manifest destiny of the past is considered preferential treatment today. The main difference is simply who the policies are aimed to support. Some may feel the arguments in this paragraph are political. To this we respond, "of course they are," just as leaving the evidence that supports these arguments out of school curricula, the news, and public consciousness is political. Why aren't many Americans aware, for example, of government practices in the 1950s that affected the distribution of $120 billion to many returning veterans, essentially created today's white middle class, and virtually excluded African Americans and other nonwhites? Who benefits by this lack of knowledge? Who is harmed? How should we compensate for this injustice? Did you know that there were legally sanctioned practices in this country that provided for the wealth accumulation of some and prevented others from the same opportunities? With higher education's ability to provide the intellectual, social, cultural, and economic capital for a better life, it seems reasonable that providing access and support for postsecondary education can be a central means for addressing past discrimination, offering equal opportunity, and promoting equity.

Policy Responses to Injustices of the Past

We turn now to policies that have evolved in this country related to equal opportunity and equitable access to higher education. In fact, there may be no better way to explore the history of social justice in postsecondary education than to trace the evolution of equal opportunity legislation and affirmative action. As we write this, the U.S. Supreme Court is preparing to hear an affirmative action case involving college admissions at the University of Texas. When this book is published, we'll be able to evaluate how well our earlier call for consciousness of history, positionality, and contemporary capital disparities are considered by the court and are evident in the larger public discourse.

Affirmative action emerged from post–*Brown v. Board of Education* (1954) desegregation movements toward civil rights and was established in 1961 in President John F. Kennedy's Executive Order 10925, which created the Committee on Equal Employment Opportunity and called for government contractors to voluntarily support affirmative action. According to Kolling (1998), however, this country did not satisfactorily respond voluntarily to efforts to ameliorate past racial biases in hiring, leading to the Civil Rights Act of 1964. For example, despite the Supreme Court's pronouncements in *Brown v. Board*, "of the 4,094 school districts in the southern and border states in 1964, more than half, enrolling more than three million black children, remained fully segregated" (Bickel, 1998, p. 6).

The Civil Rights Act of 1964 paved the way toward inclusion in higher education by providing enforcement mechanisms and assuring that federal aid would not be allocated to education institutions unless their programs provided equal educational opportunity. Title VI of the Civil Rights Act was used to push higher education to adopt admissions goals, allocate financial aid, and implement remedial programs aimed at reducing the disparity between educational attainment of black and white students (Bickel, 1998). Other civil rights legislation over the next three decades opened doors for many who had traditionally been inhibited from full participation in higher education, including Title IX of the Education Amendments of 1972 (prohibiting sex discrimination); Section 504 of the Rehabilitation Act of 1973 (prohibiting disability discrimination); Title II of the Americans with Disabilities Act of 1990 (prohibiting disability discrimination by public entities); and the Age Discrimination Act of 1975 (prohibiting age discrimination). Is it surprising that it took nearly two hundred years following the adoption of the U.S. Constitution before the people from identity groups listed earlier were provided legal protection for the rights initially guaranteed? Why did we need this legislation if the U.S. Constitution guarantees everyone equal protection? It appears that people who have been targeted for oppression and those who are social justice advocates have had to fight hard to receive the rights that past practices, policies, and procedures have prevented.

The impact of these laws through effective enforcement has helped provide access to higher education in a manner more congruent with the equity originally promised in our U.S. Constitution. The impact can be seen through the following statistics, which illustrate progress toward social justice:

• Total minority enrollment at colleges and universities increased 56 percent from 2001 to 2011 (American Council on Education, 2011).

- The percentage of American college students who are Hispanic, Asian-Pacific Islander, and black has been increasing. From 1976 to 2010, the percentage of Hispanic students rose from 3 percent to 13 percent, the percentage of Asian-Pacific Islander students rose from 2 percent to 6 percent, and the percentage of black students rose from 9 percent to 14 percent (National Center for Education Statistics, 2012).

- Between 1998 and 2008, the number of associate degrees awarded grew by 40 percent and bachelor degrees awarded grew by 41 percent. These increases were attributable to gains by every racial/ethnic group. Hispanics led all others in growth rate for both types of undergraduate degrees; in particular, the number of associate degrees awarded to Hispanics has nearly doubled in ten years. People of color received 24 percent of total bachelor's degrees awarded in 2008, up from 21 percent ten years earlier (American Council on Education, 2011).

- In 1972, prior to Title IX, 59 percent of women had at least a high school education and only 8 percent were college graduates. By 2009, 87 percent of women had a high school education and approximately 28 percent had at least a college degree (U.S. Department of Justice, 2012).

- Since Title IX, both male and female participation in high school athletics has risen: for males, from about 3.6 million in 1972 to 4.5 million in 2011, and for women, from approximately 300,000 to over 3 million in the same time period (U.S. Department of Justice, 2012).

- Nationally, the enrollment of students reporting disabilities in postsecondary institutions increased from 6 percent in 1995–96 to 11 percent in 2003–04 (National Center for Education Statistics, 2005).

Clearly, legislation to bridge the gap between what our constitution promises and what our country had historically delivered has resulted in increased access and broader inclusion. Efforts that have led to these results are not, however, without controversy. In fact, there is wide discussion both in the past and in contemporary society about the value and fairness of affirmative action. Unfortunately, much of the discourse lacks a historical perspective. For example, the week following the U.S. Supreme Court's decision to hear the *Fisher v. University of Texas* (2011) case, a Rasmussen poll indicated that most voters oppose the use of so-called affirmative action policies at colleges and universities and continue to believe those policies have not been successful (Rasmussen, 2012). While it is reasonable to oppose affirmative action, to believe that policies have not been successful in opening doors and moving toward equal rights is to ignore the wealth of data, like the statistics cited here, that prove otherwise.

Within higher education, the original legal precedent related to affirmative action was *Regents of the University of California v. Bakke* (1978). In 1974, the Supreme Court reviewed admissions policies that reserved places for disadvantaged members of certain minority groups and applied Title VI of the Civil Rights Act to establish that quota systems, where spots are reserved for a category of people, are in violation of equal opportunity law. The court affirmed, however, that racial classification was permissible as a means of overcoming the present effects of past discrimination. In addition, the specific purpose of promoting learning was established as a rationale for considering diverse backgrounds in admissions policies. Justice Powell specifically noted a school's interest in fostering the educational benefits resulting from an ethnically diverse student body when he wrote, "The attainment of a diverse student body clearly is a constitutionally permissible goal for an institution of higher education" (*Regents of the University of California v. Bakke*, 1978, p. 312). Thus, the decision upheld the principle of using race or ethnicity as a valid remediation strategy, but if colleges and universities wanted to increase racial diversity, they would have to do so without using quotas.

It wasn't until 2003 that the Supreme Court again ruled on affirmative action policies in higher education. Two cases, both involving the University of Michigan, considered policies related to undergraduate admissions (*Gratz v. Bollinger*) and its law school (*Grutter v. Bollinger*). The Supreme Court upheld the University of Michigan Law School's policy, reinforcing race as one of many factors that colleges can use to select students owing to a compelling interest in obtaining the educational benefits that flow from a diverse student body. The court, however, ruled that the formula approach used for undergraduate admissions, involving a point system awarding additional points to certain students, including some minorities, had to be modified. The undergraduate program, unlike the law school policy, did not provide the "individualized consideration" of applicants deemed necessary in previous Supreme Court decisions on affirmative action. The Supreme Court seemed to support that affirmative action was no longer valid as a strategy for rectifying past discrimination. It did, however, reaffirm that diversity is a compelling state interest and can be used in college admissions.

In addition to Supreme Court cases involving affirmative action, a policy environment has emerged in the past few decades that is defined by "a complex web of voter initiatives, judicial rulings, and gubernatorial executive orders which limit the use of affirmative action at public and private colleges" (Blume & Long, 2012, p. 2). For example, the U.S. Circuit Court decisions in *Hopwood v. Texas* (1996) prohibited the use of race or ethnicity in admissions decisions within their jurisdiction. Following the *Hopwood* decision, the Texas Attorney General issued an executive interpretation that banned affirmative action in both public colleges and private colleges that accept federal funding in Texas. The Texas legislature responded by enacting a law that guaranteed Texas high school students in the top 10 percent of their graduating class admission to any Texas public university. This policy strategy, known as a "top *x* percent" program (Long, 2004) is based on the de facto racial segregation that currently exists in most state's high schools. De facto segregation refers to the *practice* or actuality, as opposed to de jure segregation, which is codified in the *law*. The logic is that the composition of top *x* percent graduates will contain many minority students and should lead to an increase in college attendance of minority students. University of Texas at Austin announced in 2005 that it revived affirmative action (Faulkner, 2005), which has prompted the *Fisher v. University of Texas* case that is being heard by the U.S. Supreme Court as this book is being written. According to Blume and Long (2012), "the key in this case is whether the top-10% plan and other efforts have sufficiently increased diversity such that direct use of the applicant's race is unnecessary" (p. 3).

Challenges to "race-based" affirmative action have also come in the form of constitutional amendments in Arizona, California, Michigan, Nebraska, and Washington. The California electorate ended affirmative action at public institutions with the passage of Proposition 209 in 1996. In 1998, Washington State voters passed Initiative 200, which similarly banned affirmative action at public colleges and universities, using language nearly identical to Proposition 209 (Moses, Yun, & Marin, 2009). A few months later in 1999, Florida's Governor Bush signed Executive Order 99–281 to eliminate affirmative action in government employment, state contracting, and higher education admissions (Blume & Long, 2012). This initiative pushed the Board of Regents to "implement a policy prohibiting the use of racial or gender set-asides, preferences or quotas in admission to all Florida institutions of Higher Education, effectively immediately" (Bush, 1999, p. 2). Like the state legislature in Texas, the Florida Board of Regents amended their admissions policy by implementing a top *x* percent program. They guaranteed admission to the Florida state university system to the top 20 percent of public high school students (Horn & Flores, 2003). In 2001, the University of Georgia discontinued the use of race as a factor in admissions after the Eleventh Circuit Court of Appeals ruled against the use of affirmative action in *Johnson v. Board of Regents of the University of Georgia.* Voter referenda in Michigan (2006), Nebraska (2008), and Arizona (2010) produced statewide bans of affirmative action, while a similar referendum failed in Colorado in 2008. Finally, the state legislature in New Hampshire banned affirmative action for public colleges in the state in 2011 (Blume & Long, 2012). While policies like affirmative action, court cases like *Brown v. Board*, and federal legislation like the Civil Rights Act of 1964 have served to open doors for many who have historically been disenfranchised from higher education, the current political environment reflects a cacophony of serious challenges to policies that created such inclusion. Evidence suggests that higher education is more equitable and socially just than in the past, but the continued progress of such efforts is currently in question.

What Next? Ignoring the Roots of Inequality or Building Toward Equity

Today the battle lines are being drawn, and the debate over affirmative action is far from resolved. Moreover, the decision in *Fisher v. University of Texas* stands to potentially change the debate altogether. At the center of the affirmative action debate is balancing the Equal Protection Clause of the Fourteenth Amendment of the U.S. Constitution, which was approved in 1868. The Fourteenth Amendment provides that

> All persons born or naturalized in the United States, and subject to the jurisdiction thereof, are citizens of the United States and of the State wherein they reside. No State shall make or enforce any law which shall abridge the privileges or immunities of citizens of the United States; nor shall any State deprive any person of life, liberty, or property, without due process of law; nor deny to any person within its jurisdiction the equal protection of the laws [U.S. Constitution, Article XIV].

This amendment was signed into law and provides the foundation for litigation that continues today. Two clear rationales exist for maintaining race-conscious admissions policies in order to abide by the constitutional imperative of equal protection. The first is the compelling state interest in providing the educational benefits that stem from a multiculturally rich learning environment. This perspective is perhaps most clearly articulated in Justice Powell's brief in the *Bakke* (1978) decision. The second rationale is to balance off the de jure and de facto discrimination that has historically deprived many people of the equal opportunity promised in our constitution. Thus, we need to evaluate the weight of the evidence regarding both the educational benefits of diversity and the current effects of past discrimination in order to measure whether affirmative action and equal opportunity policy are providing social justice or, conversely, what some call reverse discrimination. If you were someone from an identity group who faced policies that historically inhibited your access to higher education, as described throughout this chapter, how would you feel about opposition to polices that now provide access like affirmative action? If you were unaware of historical limits on access, how would you feel about race- or class-conscious policies?

Educational Benefits of Diversity

The educational benefits of diversity are characterized by John Stuart Mill, in his famous essay *On Liberty* (1859), in which he provides a convincing rationale for submitting popular opinions to the marketplace of ideas. He persuasively argues that any culture seeking intellectual advancement needs to be aware of how perceptions are narrowed by the biases inherent in the limited views people develop based on experience, education, class, or other backgrounds. In fact, one could argue that the biases that shaped the discriminatory policies that gave rise to the need for affirmative action emerged from just such a situation.

In other words, those making policies have historically represented relatively homogenous demographic backgrounds, which provides one reason for the discriminatory practices discussed earlier in this chapter. How does your background or position both facilitate and inhibit your perspective and understanding? It would be instructive for readers to see how much of this homogeneity of backgrounds remains true today in all three branches of federal government. How many presidents have been nonwhite? How many members of Congress are women or are gay? What religious affiliations and social class backgrounds have been represented on the Supreme Court? In response to the judicial branch's establishing the legitimacy of affirmative action to create diverse learning environments, the American Council on Education (ACE, 2002) studied the issue and developed a set of statements supporting diversity in higher education. ACE states that diversity (a) enriches the educational experience, (b) promotes personal growth and a healthy society, (c) strengthens communities and the workplace, and (d) enhances American's economic competitiveness (Litolff, 2007). While these principles seem logical and appropriate, they need to be vetted through research regarding the effects of diversity in education.

Astin (1993) examined the impact of college on student outcomes with 24,847 students from 217 different institutions and found that students from all racial and ethnic backgrounds benefit from institutions that have a visible commitment to diversity. Institutional goals or policies to increase representation of people from diverse backgrounds positively affected student's self-reported growth in cultural awareness and their commitment to racial understanding. Commitment to a multicultural learning context also had a positive effect on student satisfaction and the overall college experience. Participating in discussions about ethnic issues had a positive effect on students' critical thinking abilities, analytical and problem-solving skills, and writing proficiency. Results suggest that "inclusion of students from diverse populations and backgrounds provides opportunities for students to hear a variety of perspectives about race and ethnic issues. In turn, exposure to diverse perspectives enhances the cognitive development of students" (Schuford, 1998, p. 73).

Supporting Astin's (1993) findings, Loes, Pascarella, and Umbach (2012) examined 3,081 students spanning nineteen institutions of higher education and found that white students and students with relatively low levels of tested academic preparation (like the ACT) in particular derived substantial critical thinking benefits from engagement in interactional diversity activities. Their analysis led them to conclude that "engagement in diversity experiences may have important implications for the intellectual development of substantial numbers of students during the first year of college ... [and] an institutional policy based on programmatic efforts to weave exposure to diverse individuals, ideas, and perspectives into students' lives may serve to enhance the intellectual mission of a college" (Loes et al., 2012, p. 21).

Milem (2003) similarly described the wealth of not only individual benefits, but a wide array of institutional, private sector, and civic benefits of racial diversity in higher education. Individual benefits included enhancing critical and complex thinking ability, enhancing the ability to understand diverse perspectives, providing greater satisfaction with the college experience, increasing student persistence, improving the racial and cultural awareness of students, increasing a commitment to racial understanding, providing a more supportive campus racial climate, and increasing wages for graduates. Institutional benefits included a more student-centered approach to teaching and learning, greater diversity in curricular offerings, more research focused on issues of race/ethnicity and gender, and more women and faculty of color involved in community and volunteer service. The economic benefits included the cultivation of a workforce with greater levels of cross-cultural competence, a greater available talent pool, enhanced marketing efforts, higher levels of creativity and innovation, better problem-solving abilities, and greater organizational flexibility.

Societal benefits included decreased occupational and residential segregation, greater engagement socially and politically, decreased stereotyping, higher levels of community service, increased equity in society, and a more educated citizenry. In sum, Milem's work demonstrates the need for greater diversity based upon the benefits to individuals, institutions, and society.

In a study where major affirmative action in higher education Supreme Court cases took place, Gurin, Nagada, and Lopez (2004) conducted a longitudinal survey of students at the University of Michigan. As in previous research, this study empirically identified and supported the educational benefits of diversity. The Gurin et al. (2004) study concluded that student diversity has the potential to provide a positive educational experience for students and results in a host of positive learning outcomes. Gurin et al. summarized:

> The discrepancy that racial and ethnic diversity on college campuses offers students for personal development and preparation for citizenship in an increasingly multicultural society depends on actual experience that students have with diverse peers. Just as positive educational benefits of racial and ethnic desegregation depended on real integration of children from different backgrounds, higher education institutions have to make use of racial/ethnic diversity by creating educational programs that bring diverse students together in meaningful, civil discourse to learn from each other [p. 32].

Quite simply, the benefits of diversity on a wide range of college outcomes have been well documented by these studies and many others (for example, Chang, Astin, & Kim, 2004; Chang, Denson, Saenz, & Misa, 2006; Gurin, Dey, Hurtado, & Gurin, 2002; Hu & Kuh, 2003; Hurtado, 2001; Jayakumar, 2008; Kuklinski, 2006; Milem, 2003; Pascarella & Terenzini, 2005). The full results of affirmative action policies in terms of access and retention are, however, less than clear. While research has shown that affirmative action has had a substantially positive impact on increasing the racial diversity of colleges, the educational achievement of many underrepresented students, and the distribution of gains resulting from higher education in the population (Bowen & Bok, 1998; Epple, Romano, & Sieg, 2008), it also has suggested disparities in who benefits. For example, Brown, Langer, and Stewart (2012) studied the effects of affirmative action policies across the globe and found that policies directed primarily toward basic education may reduce intragroup inequality, but policies concerning higher education "are likely to improve the position of those who are already the elite within the poor group, or to create an elite, in both cases worsening intra-group inequality" (p. 25). In addition, it appears that although public discourse focuses on preferential treatment based on race or ethnicity, white women have been the primary beneficiaries of affirmative action policies, both in higher education and the larger society.

Postracial America?

The myth that ethnic minorities are the face of preferential treatment is one of the reasons why we focus on race-based oppression in this historical discussion of social justice in higher education. It is important, however, to remember that systemic hurdles remain intact based on other targeted identities like sexual orientation, religion, disability, and so on. Just as these identity dimensions are intersectional, so are systems of oppression. In this chapter, race is being used as an example of and gateway to engage other systems of oppression.

While there is little ambiguity in the research regarding the benefits of diversity to the goals of higher education, it is more difficult to clearly portray convincing evidence of the present effects of past discrimination. It is more difficult for several reasons.

First, some will look at the severity of past discrimination (like lynching) and compare it to current racism (like hiring decisions) and downplay the current impact. Second, some will look at a few exemplars and make claims that ignore the larger picture. John McWhorter (2008), writing for *Forbes*, for example, epitomizes both of these perspectives when he writes:

> Our proper concern is not whether racism still exists, but whether it remains a serious problem. The election of Obama proved, as nothing else could have, that it no longer does. I make that claim while quite sure that in 2009, a noose or three will be hung somewhere, some employer will be revealed to have used the N-word on tapes of a meeting, and so on. America will remain imperfect, as humans have always been. It's not an accident, however, that increasingly, alleged cases of racism are tough calls, reflecting the complexity of human affairs rather than the stark injustice of Jim Crow [p. 1].

Can the election of a single multiracial person to the U.S. presidency mean that racism no longer exists or is no longer a serious problem? Is someone hanging a noose or using the N word simply a reflection of "the complexity of human affairs"? A third difficulty in measuring current effects of past discrimination is the ease of alternative explanations for the kind of racism present today. Dinesh D'Souza, past president of The King's College, authored a book entitled *The End of Racism: Principles for a Multiracial Society* in 1996, in which he essentially points to moral decay and relativism as the problems that keep various ethnic groups oppressed, rather than institutional racism. Ignoring the legal discrimination described earlier in this chapter and the wealth of policies and practices that have limited opportunities to nonwhites, D'Souza portrays an all-too-acceptable "perfectly logical explanation." We also outlined earlier in this chapter why promoting justice requires one to be conscious of his or her position in relationship to historical events. We would argue that it is unsurprising that someone from D'Souza's economic and cultural background would be blind to the racism encountered on a daily basis by many in this country. A 2004 study, for example, illustrated that those with African American–sounding names were significantly discriminated against compared to those with white-sounding names in job searches. Bertrand and Mullainathan (2004) performed a well-designed study that placed help-wanted ads in Boston and Chicago newspapers and found that white-sounding names receive 50 percent more callbacks for interviews with all other factors controlled. This scholarly evidence illustrates contemporary labor market racism, not laziness, moral decay, relativism, or any other perfectly logical explanation.

In spite of both historical and contemporary evidence of racism, there seems to be momentum behind removing race-conscious policies in higher education. Some call for eliminating racial categories in favor of using socioeconomic class. While this may seem like a good idea on its face, conflating class and race will not solve the problem of racial inequality in higher education. According to Byrd, Reed, and Graves (2011), "low socioeconomic status has not been the basis for systematic exclusion of students from higher education; race and ethnicity have [and] money does not shelter people from racism" (p. 1). Moreover, Kane's (1998) twelve-year longitudinal study found that class cannot be substituted for race in admission without having substantially negative effects on campus diversity. According to Kane, in order for a college to achieve a substantial enrollment of ethnically underrepresented students without considering race as a factor, "it would have to reserve six times as many places for low-income students as it now reserves for minority students" (1998, p. 25). Karabel (1998) similarly found, in a review of data on all California seniors taking the SAT, that the main beneficiaries of an admission policy emphasizing class would be low-income whites and Asians, thereby doing little to maintain the diversity called for in a quality educational experience.

Given the complexities in raising consciousness about the present effects of past discrimination, difficulties in making the case, and the wealth of data supporting the educational value of a rich representation of ethnicities on campus, we agree with those who argue for focusing on the mandate for diversity as an educational outcome. Individuals who enhance the diversity for a particular campus are admitted not because they are deficient (due to past discrimination) but because the larger campus population is deficient in its diversity (Cahn, 1997). For example, a Catholic college like St. John's in Collegeville, Minnesota, might benefit from the preferential admission of Jewish and Muslim students, and a historically black university like Morehouse might enhance its educational mission by affirmatively admitting white students.

We believe there are many creative ways to provide opportunities in a manner congruent with equal opportunity and social justice. Unfortunately, those unaware of history appear doomed to repeat it. Research illustrates that if race-based affirmative action is outlawed, it will have a deleterious impact on the ability of colleges and universities to maintain a diverse student body (Moreno, 2003). In fact, data show that underrepresented student enrollments at many of the most prestigious public universities have dropped significantly since policies banning race-based affirmative action passed. At University of California–Berkeley, for example, Latino first-year enrollments dropped from over 15 percent to less than 8 percent in the two years immediately following the ban, and during the same time African American enrollments dropped from 6 percent to slightly less than 4 percent. In 2010, African Americans represented just 2 percent of the first-year students (Kahlenberg, 2012a). Similarly, University of Michigan had African American first-year enrollments of 9 percent in 2001, but following *Grutter v. Bollinger* African Americans represented less than 5 percent of the entering class in 2010 (Kahlenberg, 2012a). Rolling back affirmative action programs runs the risk of recreating a segregated higher education system where black and Hispanic students attend less selective colleges, while whites and Asians attend more selective upper-tier institutions. We agree with Justice Blackmun in the Supreme Court's 1978 *Bakke* case, where he wrote:

> I suspect that it would be impossible to arrange an affirmative action program in a racially neutral way and have it successful. To ask that this be so is to demand the impossible. In order to get beyond racism, we must first take account of race. There is no other way. And in order to treat some persons equally, we must treat them differently. We cannot—dare not—let the Equal Protection Clause perpetuate racial supremacy.

As we will discuss in more detail in the following chapter, equity demands sometimes that we treat people differently. Equal opportunity does not exist in a vacuum, but is historically situated and culturally mediated.

Conclusion

History has a critical role to play in social justice education and practice. History deepens and informs policies and practices, particularly because many have not paid enough attention to the historical evidence that adds perspective on the need for social justice in higher education to realize the promises outlined in our constitution. A central tenet of this book is that employing a social justice–focused practice requires us to always ask what historical evidence remains covered up and whose voices or perspectives are not being heard. Zinn (1990) states, "there is an underside to every age about which history does not often speak, because history is written from records left by the privileged" (p. 102). To effectively promote learning, the central outcome of higher education, we will need to move from educational interventions that require memorization of "facts" and "truths" to learning that immerses students in controversies, requires them to find competing evidence, empowers them to develop critical thinking skills that question interpretations, and prepares them to develop their own arguments based on reputable evidence. Loewen (1995) suggests that "citizens who are their own historians, willing to identify lies and distortions and able to use sources to determine what really went on in the past, become a formidable force for democracy" (p. 318).

Another tenet of the book is to ask who benefits and what is the economic impact of our policies. Many assume, for example, that we live in a society where race no longer matters. As this book will clearly illustrate, if we move away from political pundits and commercial news outlets and look at hard evidence, we will find that the economic indicators clearly illustrate unequal outcomes that are tightly correlated with ethnicity and the historical oppression of certain groups. For example, if you were to compare ethnic diversity based on admissions data compared to persistence or graduation statistics, what would you find? What portion of federal funds for education are directed toward postsecondary schools that recruit underrepresented students, charge high tuition, and have graduation rates at less than 30 percent?

Also central to this book is a focus on "doing social justice" that requires both active engagement in debate and practice and a willingness to engage with others in ways that honor academic rather than political correctness. The arts of inquiry and civil debate sometimes appear lost in the avalanche of puppet news outlets, well-funded political misinformation campaigns, and talk show demagogues. While we will be outlining strategies for engaging in civil disagreement and scholarly debate, for now it is important to remember that the history many have been taught does not include facts that support the need for affirmative action and social justice intervention. The histories described in Loewen (1999, 1995), Takaki (1993), Solomon (1985), and Zinn (1990, 2005) are generally not taught in high school or even college. Should we really be surprised when educated people lack the historical understanding that is so critical to comprehending why social justice aims are important? While it's sometimes shocking when we confront those who are unaware of the injustices waged in this country, our educational processes can slip into dogmatic debate if we forget that sometimes the heart of ignorance is not malicious intent, but routine hegemony. Inviting students to find out for themselves and teaching them critical intellectual skills is much more effective in our experience than debating the existence of a reality that has been constructed through a matrix of culturally embedded narratives. Anchoring students in an accurate and more comprehensive understanding of history achieved through self-discovery, listening to the voices of those typically left out of the stories, and development of essential inquiry skills can put people on the road to the kind of critical consciousness necessary for effective social justice practice.

4

Critical Pedagogy

The Foundation of Social Justice Educational Practice

To teach is not to transfer knowledge but to create the possibilities for the production or construction of knowledge.
—Paulo Freire (2001, p. 30)

It is important that students come to grips with what a given society has made of them, how it has incorporated them ideologically and materially into its rules and logic, and what it is that they need to affirm and reject in their own histories in order to begin the process of struggling for the conditions that will give them opportunities to lead a self-managed existence.
—Henry Giroux (2009, p. 47)

While a conceptual and historical basis for addressing social justice is critical for effective practice, knowledge alone will not effect change. The nexus between the two maxims, "don't just sit there, do something" and "don't just do something, sit there" is a critical pedagogy consciously implemented. We believe that those conscious of historical disparities that foreground the contemporary gaps between what our democracy promises and what is realized will be moved to action. In this chapter we attempt to inform the construction of a foundation upon which to develop social justice educational practice. We've defined social justice action as efforts to bridge the gap between what our U.S. Constitution demands and the lived reality of many people, with a focus on equal participation in decision making and equitable distribution of resources. College and university mission statements can similarly be evaluated in terms of social justice when people raise questions about whether behaviors are congruent with stated beliefs. Divestiture of university investments in South Africa during apartheid is an example of social justice efforts in higher education to align mission with actions. While investing in South Africa under apartheid was legal, many found that doing so was incongruent with higher education's mission to educate toward democracy, and therefore unjust. Critical pedagogy adds a dimension to such challenges by centering "the empowerment of culturally marginalized and economically disenfranchised students" (Darder, Baltodano, & Torres, 2009, p. 9). Social justice efforts are sometimes necessary when institutional members and decision makers are seduced away from their missions through financial incentives, private interests, or other benefits. More often, however, challenges to integrity emerge from hidden hegemonies, slow erosion of purpose through seemingly innocuous assimilative acts, and uncritically accepted appearances (for example, partial truths and myths) that are assumed to be essences (such as truth and reality). In order to practice in a manner that promotes social justice, then, a method of critically analyzing decisions, policies, practices, and procedures is required. Strategies to uncover hidden hegemonies, interrupt blind assimilation, and question whether essences are consistent with appearance are necessary for healthy individual and cultural growth, as well as social justice. Critical pedagogy, buttressed by critical theory, is offered as a framework for raising such questions because of its recursive, context-illuminating, and dialectic demands.

The central feature of critical pedagogy, though there are many that will be described throughout this chapter, is its dialectical nature. Dialectical education not only explores tensions among relevant concepts, but also seeks to expose the various ways knowledge is constructed. As discussed in Chapter Two, dialectical understanding "seeks to free knowledge production from the authoritarian explanations of the certified experts" (Kincheloe, 2005, p. 23). Rather than rely solely on the perspectives of others, to be critical requires us to participate in and not be a passive recipient of the knowledge production process. It actually makes some sense, when we consider cognitive development theory, that we naturally develop a deeply docile reliance on experts for their version of the truth as we initially assume that truth resides "out there" in their constructions. Our behavior as learners in this cognitive developmental stage, described by Perry (1970) as "dualism," is to receive knowledge from experts and memorize the concepts they teach us. However, a cognitively mature individual develops complexity that requires first an awareness that "truth" is relative and then initiates a critical process in which an internalized evaluative system is developed and used to filter knowledge. Critical pedagogy, similarly, involves the following:

- Understanding the socially constructed nature of knowledge

- Illuminating the historical, economic, and other factors that influence knowledge

- Exposing the processes by which certain information is validated or invalidated

- Focusing on personal experiences of the knower and similar learning strategies that inspire knower participation in the construction of knowledge

- Ultimately aiming toward self-authorship and liberation of all members of society

Each of these facets of critical pedagogy will be discussed in the paragraphs that follow, but it is important to recognize that just as there is no one universally accepted critical theory, critical pedagogy takes many forms. In fact, according to Darder et al. (2009), "it is precisely this distinguishing factor that constitutes its critical nature, and therefore its most emancipatory and democratic function" (p. 9). In other words, critical pedagogy maintains integrity by functioning *between* any dogmatic definition (received knowledge) and the knower. Tensions among heterogeneous concepts and the diverse ways in which critical pedagogy can be implemented demand that we breathe life into the theoretical by both reconciling conceptual conflicts and integrating them into our personal philosophical framework. Our own critical perspectives are informed by Paulo Freire's foundational scholarship on emancipatory education, which questions the powers, cultures, and oppressions that inhibit human agency and democratic participation. The earliest use of the term *critical pedagogy* of which we are aware was by Henry Giroux (1983) in *Theory and Resistance in Education*, and we are influenced by his thinking and other critical scholars like Peter McLaren, bell hooks, Michelle Fine, Stephen Brookfield, and Antonia Darder. We also use perspectives of Gramsci and Foucault, particularly with regard to hegemony and power, respectively. While we are familiar with the Frankfurt School of critical theorists and are influenced by several, especially Marcuse, our leanings at this point in our lives are slightly less focused on these insightful scholars' Marxist orientation. We share, furthermore, McLaren's (2009) view that "critical theorists begin with the premise that men and women are essentially unfree and inhabit a world rife with contradictions and asymmetries of power and privilege" (p. 61). In the tradition of critical theory, we share our position here to illuminate our influences and assumptions about critical pedagogy. Readers are encouraged to use this chapter in conjunction with other critical perspectives in order to continually develop a personal pedagogy that works in synch with your own theoretical leanings, epistemological assumptions, and interpersonal style, but also incorporates the central concepts that follow.

Social Construction

Since critical pedagogy requires one to participate in the production of knowledge, it is crucial to begin with an understanding of the various philosophical assumptions about what constitutes knowledge. As described in Chapter One, those taking a positivist epistemological perspective assume that truth exists objectively in the external world, that the rational scientific approach can remove subjectivity in order to analyze reality, and that one can understand complex phenomena best by reducing them to their parts and piecing elements back together according to causal principles (Kincheloe, 2005). In direct opposition to positivists, generally, constructivists believe that truth is socially constructed and what we know always involves a knower whose filter of knowledge is built upon historical, cultural, and other subjective experiences and understandings. The constructivist perspective, articulated by Piaget (1954) and Vygotsky (1978), and widely accepted today, suggests that knowledge does not and cannot produce representations of an independent reality, but instead is rooted in the perspective of the knower. Meaning is constructed as we engage the world and interpret it and, as such, knowledge and truth cannot exist independently from context.

The social construction of knowledge resonates with us as teachers and student affairs professionals. Students come to class or to educational interventions with a wide range of differences, not just in terms of academic preparation or intellectual skill, but also with a diversity of cultural, economic, and identity-based experiences that shape what they hear and subsequently learn. If we accepted a positivist position, we would simply lecture the "objective truth" and expect those lacking "the truth" to memorize it or otherwise passively learn it. What we've discovered, however, is that students come to class with extant worldviews based on their experiences. We believe, like Aronowitz (2001), that "education takes place when there are two learners who occupy somewhat different spaces in an ongoing dialogue (and) one of the objectives of the pedagogic process is to explore what each knows and what they can teach each other" (p. 8). Not only do our students come with complex lived experiences that shape their knowledge, we as educators are steeped in epistemological assumptions and theoretical bases upon which our pedagogies emerge. As anyone who has traveled to a different culture has learned, there can be multiple perspectives on the same reality. The movie *Rashomon* (Jingo & Kurosawa, 1950) or the more recent critically acclaimed *Tucker & Dale vs. Evil* (Eden Rock Media & Craig, 2011) powerfully illustrate the different perspectives that people can have related to the same exact phenomenon. What appears absurd in one culture is standard in another, what social behavior calls attention to in one goes unnoticed or is seen as completely natural in another. It's important here to clarify that this sort of *cultural relativism* should not be conflated with *moral relativism,* as some too often do—that is, the fact that knowledge is subjective does not provide intellectual license for doing whatever we want. On the contrary, cultural relativism and knowledge subjectivity require anyone engaged in balancing rights, morals, and social justice to consider how their own enculturation shapes their understanding.

The importance of social construction and multiple perspectives to social justice is that the separation of expert and student, or knower and known, "produces a hidden logic of domination between teacher-student, researcher-researched, and knower-known; not content to occupy only the terrain of inquiry, this logic trespasses into the domain of race, class and gender relations" (Kincheloe, 2005, p. 15). Wherever duality is constructed, the empowerment of one and denigration of the other is possible. Consider, for example, one's perspective on the recurring Middle East conflict between Israel and the Palestinians. To some people, the Palestinian Liberation Organization represents freedom fighters; to others, they are terrorists. The same is true for Israeli forces. To some degree this difference depends on where you were born and what your lived experiences were. Further illustrating the historically contextual nature of knowledge is the fact that the U.S. government has identified individuals as terrorists who were formerly allies.

Another important factor in connecting social justice to the social construction of knowledge, in addition to dissolving the artificial and hierarchical duality constructed in positivism, is empowering learners to begin cultivating their own voices and envisioning their own response-abilities in the production of knowledge. Rather than passively receiving the knowledge sold to them by teachers, parents, religious institutions, commercial interests, and other "masters of the universe," students begin to develop critical consumer skills that can lead to authoring their own lives in a more personally authentic manner. This is not to say that the received knowledge taught by teachers, parents, religious leaders, or other sources of information is necessarily good or bad, right or wrong. Rather, consciousness, critical thinking, and human liberation require that these dogmas are reconsidered and routinely exposed for the cataleptic conceptual doctrine that has served them during a time prior to taking on the mental demands of adulthood and citizenship (Kegan, 1994). These new intellectual, interpersonal, and intrapersonal demands upon which higher education is built require learners to breathe new life into their passively received meaning-making framework in order to reconstruct their own authentic foundation.

Historical, Political, and Economic Influences on Knowledge Production

The constructivist position that calls learners to participate in the creation and recreation of knowledge also recognizes that history and political-economic conditions shape how meaning is made. Historical events shape knowledge and educational practice by providing boundaries to what seems possible and orienting one toward sanctioned norms, values, and what are considered appropriate behaviors. For example, many scholars who research and write about generational influences (Coomes & DeBard, 2004; Howe & Strauss, 2000; Twenge, 2006) suggest that when people were born shapes them at least as much as where they were born or who their parents were. Consider the social milieu during tough economic periods compared to that of boom economies. Those living through the Great Depression, for example, view saving and spending money quite differently from those who have not been exposed to such history. Similarly, it makes sense that people coming of age during the Civil Rights era of the 1950s and 1960s see the world and construct knowledge a little differently from those born in the 1980s. War, acts of terrorism, national tragedies, economic conditions, common celebrations, and other historical events can shape what is taught, what is considered undiscussable, and thus how knowledge is constructed. Students who consciously apply this view begin to see themselves as subjects of history and "to recognize that conditions of injustice, although historically produced by human beings, can also be transformed by human beings" (Darder et al., 2009, p. 11).

Critical theory contends that, like history, economic interests and marketplace ideology influence schools and the production of knowledge. A central tenet of critical pedagogy is therefore to unveil and analyze the structural relationships and policies that reproduce class interests, particularly those that are aimed at oppressing the least politically and economically powerful. In my (Davis's) classroom teaching, for example, when students discuss educational policies or hypothesize about why certain decisions are made, I encourage them to ask questions like "what would we discover if we followed the money?" or "who benefits economically from this decision?" For example, when U.S. slavery is discussed, many students believe there was a deep-seated racism and hatred toward "black" Africans that served as a rationale for their enslavement. I challenge them to consider the economic benefits of African slavery that provided free labor and the skin pigmentation that made it easier to identify who was a slave and who was not. This is not to say that there are not other factors, like a deeply colonial mentality of landowners that influenced U.S. slavery—the point is that students are challenged to include an economic or market interest perspective in their analysis.

A contemporary example of economic influence on the production of knowledge is the current commodification of public education by private commerce. Current conceptions of the purposes of higher education focus too exclusively on supporting corporate interests and market forces. From the naming rights of athletic arenas to exclusive soda contracts to huge entrepreneurial research grants, corporate influence is challenging the fundamental purposes of education. Miller (2003), for example, argues that "academic institutions have come to resemble the entities they now serve; colleges have been transformed into big businesses. Major research schools, particularly private ones, are also landlords, tax havens, and research-and-development surrogates, with administrators and fund-raisers lording it over faculty" (p. 902). The original goals of developing critical capacities and citizenship education have taken a back seat to commercial interests. Similarly, as contemporary secondary education teachers well know, public schools focus extensively on quantitative high-stakes testing at the expense of developing of critically minded and engaged democratic citizens. Barber (1995) asks, "What does it say about our civic commitment to public schools and their students that issues of democracy, social justice, and critical thinking have largely disappeared from school curricula, which is now increasingly determined by test preparations?" (p. xvii). The historical purposes of education include preparing students to be active participants in democracy, promoting disciplinary knowledge and critical thinking skills, enhancing abilities to lead successful lives, and training to participate in our economy. While these facets of a liberal education are still alive today—to a greater degree in some institutional types than others—higher education faces threats of being reduced to a political economy of commercial interests, vocational training, and technical skill development.

Hegemony and Power: Exposing How Knowledge Is Validated or Invalidated

Hegemony refers to the way in which social control is carried out by the dominant ruling class to protect its interests. Antonio Gramsci (2000) suggests that rather than the need for violence, hegemony is a process of influence where people willingly consent to political decisions, economic interests, and even pedagogical techniques that serve to reinforce the status quo, thereby protecting the privileged and continuing to disenfranchise the culturally marginalized. This happens through a normalizing process in which a particular way of comprehending social reality is fabricated or forged through ideas, language, perspectives, theories, and other forms of discourse and these become so embedded that they are accepted as common sense or as part of the natural order.

In my (Davis's) research on gender and male-identified students, for example, I have seen how men will literally fight to defend a set of regulations related to traditional masculine ideology that are essentially harmful to their own well-being. For instance, I've seen men ignore health symptoms, drink themselves into oblivion, and get into physical altercations in order to maintain the appearance of toughness, emotional control, and to avoid appearing "feminine." The power of hegemony lies not only in its ability to fabricate a particular way of comprehending reality, but also in the fact that there seems little chance for opposing it. When a concept is seen as naturally occurring (for example, biological explanations of gender roles) and is reinforced by daily lived experience, challenging it with alternative possibilities becomes particularly difficult. According to Brookfield (2005), "ideology becomes hegemony when the dominant ideas are learned and lived in everyday decisions and judgments and when these ideas (reinforced by the mass media images and messages) pervade the whole existence" (p. 94). Another feature of hegemony is that it isn't necessary to exert hierarchical power to gain consent; rather, the matrix or system is "mediated by well-intentioned people who, usually unconsciously, act as agents of oppression by merely going about their daily lives" (Bell & Griffin, 1997, p. 10). In the United States, Christian norms, rituals, rules, and language presume the almost exclusive existence of Protestant or Catholic faiths. Christian privilege is hidden through symbols, holiday celebrations, media-focused attention, and even public school vacations that largely ignore the existence of Buddhist, Muslim, Jewish, or other possibilities of religiousness. I have a friend, for example, whose kindergarten-aged son came home from school one day riddled with guilt because he raised his hand when the teacher asked "who celebrates Christmas?" As a Muslim, he didn't want to lie, but felt even greater fear of not following along like everyone else. This act by the teacher is presumably well intentioned, yet it was carried out in a manner that reinforces Christian hegemony. Extreme examples of religious oppression might gain attention, but the everyday insults, exclusions, and marginalizing actions endured by non-Christians remain hidden to most. Sue (2010) describes these everyday, subtle ways in which people experience hostility and discrimination, whether intentioned or not, as microaggressions. Though each incident by itself may seem insignificant, their accumulated frequency adds up to a much larger impact.

In addition to hegemony, Foucault's (1980) description of power relationships and how "regimes of truth" are legitimized sheds additional light onto how certain interests are maintained and reproduced. Power relations are constructed through discourses or sets of regulating statements and maintained through discursive practices. Discursive practices are essentially "rules that govern what can be said and what must remain unsaid, who can speak with authority and who must listen" (McLaren, 2009, p. 72). In a student affairs classroom setting, for example, dominant educational discourses and professional discursive practices determine what books are used, what pedagogies are employed, and what values are transmitted to students. A more specific example of discursive educational practices offered earlier in this book was how relatively conservative discourses constructed history lessons in books where wealthy white Christian men were centered. A liberal discourse would argue for inclusion of historical perspectives of women and those from minoritized populations. A critical discourse, the kind we advocate in this chapter, would raise questions about whose interests are represented, how socioeconomic inequality influences historical representation, and how our current contextual position directs the shaping of knowledge. The key point is that dominant discourses determine what counts as true and important. According to Foucault (1980),

> Truth is a thing of this world: it is produced only by virtue of multiple forms of constraint. And it induces regular effects of power. Each society has its regime of truth, its "general politics" of truth: that is, the types of discourse which it accepts and makes function as true; the mechanisms and instances which enable one to distinguish true and false statements, the means by which each is sanctioned; the techniques and procedures accorded value in the acquisition of truth; the status of those who are charged with saying what counts as true [p. 131].

Thus, truth is established and policed by those with power. Challenges to established ideologies are generally met with significant resistance.

While we absorb various forms of hegemony and learn to police others' behaviors toward conformity, we also have the capacity to become critically aware of how cultural and economic domination occurs and to develop consciousness so that we transform our culture and facilitate human liberation through resistance, critique, and counterhegemonic social action. Questions to raise in implementing a critical pedagogy, according to Kincheloe (2005) include: "How does the existence of socio-economic inequality along the lines of race, class, gender, sexuality, religion and language influence our answers to these educational questions? What happens to our answers when we bring an understanding of power to our analytical table? What is the effect of social theoretical insight on the subjectivity and context-dependency of knowledge production?" (p. 4). In addition, centering the voices and stories of those who have historically existed in the margins of higher education can provide counternarratives that resist the reproduction of status quo interests. Shaun Harper's outstanding research on successful African American men stands as an example of effective counternarrative disruption of racism (Harper & Davis, 2012; Harper, 2009). It is very important, however, for critical educators to understand critique as an ongoing process. According to Darder et al. (2009), "each time a radical form threatens the integrity of the status quo, generally this element is appropriated, stripped of its transformative intent, and reified into a palatable form" (p. 12). Like the dialectical view of knowledge described earlier, critical pedagogy does not rest with one answer, but rather demands a constant, dynamic, recursive questioning of tentatively arrived-at positions.

From Masks of Ideology to Critical Consciousness

For Freire (2000), education is never an impersonal or neutral act, but an intensely humanistic and intimate interaction guided by methodological rigor, ethical commitment, respect for the autonomy of the student, capacity to be critical, driving curiosity, awareness of being unfinished, and a deep-seated hope and joy in human capacity to change. In this chapter so far we have explored mainly conceptual frameworks related to knowledge: how it is socially constructed, the historical and political-economic influence on it, and how it is validated through hegemony and power. In order to bring theory to practice, we need to faithfully engage in processes that manifest the conceptual. Freire (2000) outlines the central process for a critical pedagogy that inspires social justice: "Critical reflection on practice is a requirement of the relationship between theory and practice. Otherwise theory becomes simply 'blah, blah, blah,' and practice, pure activism" (p. 30). The Freirean notion of praxis, then, is a combination of action and reflection in order to promote social justice. As outlined earlier in the chapter, such critical reflection needs to be focused on the social, economic, and cultural conditions that bear on the educational process.

In addition to such critical reflection on institutional forces, enacting critical pedagogy requires the mindful awareness of the human influences on learning. There is no substitute for listening deeply to and striving to understand the stories and histories of those with whom we engage in a learning-developmental process. Listening mindfully means being open to the word and world of the other. Doing so not only serves as an inoculation against projecting our own ideologies onto someone else, it also inspires the sort of empathy necessary for considering alternative histories that shape the other's construction of knowledge. According to Freire (2000), "those who have something to say should know that they are not the only ones with ideas and opinions that need to be expressed (and) that if this is not taken into account, their talking, no matter how correct and convincing, will not fall on receptive ears" (p. 105). As clearly illustrated in the earlier discussion of the social construction of knowledge, the personal experiences of the knower implicitly affect learning. Listening, asking questions about personal experiences, and the resulting dialogue not only offer potential to build the relationship necessary for transformative learning, they also instruct the educator about how the student has constructed knowledge and thus reveal the most effective methods for forming an educational intervention. Alvarez (2009), for example, challenges us to consider Chaucer's Wife of Bath, who "reminds us, 'Who peynte the leon, tel me who?' In other words, if the picture of the hunter slaying a lion had been painted by the lion, what would the scene look like? What would an education look like that includes both the lion's and the hunter's point of view?" (p. xxiii). How can we prepare educators for a pluralistic world if we do not do justice to the pluralism they will encounter? Asking questions and listening also moves us toward preserving the autonomy of the learner and focuses our attention on cultivating the conditions where students actively participate in the construction of knowledge.

This form of critical pedagogy, with its reliance on questioning, listening, and dialogue, serves as an antidote to the kind of banking system of education described by Freire (1970, 1985, 2000). Under the pretense of neutrality and technical rationalism of a positivist epistemology, the banking system assumes

- The teacher teaches and the students are taught

- The teacher knows everything and the students know nothing

- The teacher thinks and the students are thought about

- The teacher talks and the students listen—meekly

- The teacher disciplines and the students are disciplined

- The teacher chooses and enforces his choice, and the students comply

- The teacher acts and the students have the illusion of acting through the action of the teacher

- The teacher chooses the program content, and the students (who were not consulted) adapt to it

- The teacher confuses the authority of knowledge with his or her own professional authority, which she and he sets in opposition to the freedom of the students

- The teacher is the Subject of the learning process, while the pupils are mere objects (Freire, 1970, p. 59)

While these assumptions and behaviors are evident in primary and secondary schools, we routinely see university professors and other college educators operating from this same perspective. In contrast to the banking metaphor, where knowledge is deposited in a passive recipient, critical pedagogy is more accurately conceived as an act of mature love where the relationship is mutually negotiated, ego is subdued by the recognition and appreciation of another's value, and there exists a healthy balance between interpersonal, intrapersonal, and cognitive influences.

Thus, the kind of critical pedagogy advocated in this book calls for a sort of yin-yang approach that stimulates deeply rational critical facilities which integrate historical, political, and economic context while simultaneously kindling the deeply emotional human capacities for empathy, compassion, and curiosity. In order to manifest a truly effective critical pedagogy, educators need to dissolve the artificially constructed dualism between cognition and emotion, interpersonal and intrapersonal, object and subject, and bring these into dialectical consideration. According to Freire (1970), "apart from inquiry, apart from the praxis, individuals cannot be truly human. Knowledge emerges only through invention and re-invention, through the restless, impatient, continuing, hopeful inquiry human beings pursue in the world, with the world, and with each other" (p. 58). This form of dialectical reciprocity is fundamental to critical pedagogy.

If one were to honor the key tenets of a Freirean-style critical pedagogy, he or she could develop a social consciousness of the complex realities of how knowledge is constructed, sold, and maintained. Those following the positivist epistemological perspective view knowledge construction as a banking system and see reality in only partial fragments that are not accurately understood as constituent elements of the whole. Like those chained to the wall in Plato's allegory of the cave, they remain unconscious of the critical influences beyond their sight and do not know that they do not know. In the cave allegory, Socrates describes a group of people who have lived chained to the wall of a cave all of their lives, facing a blank wall. They observe shadows projected on the wall by artifacts passing in front of a fire behind them, and ascribe forms or "truths" to these shadows. According to Plato's Socrates, the shadows are as close as the prisoners get to seeing reality. Those developing awareness of the social construction of knowledge are like those who are chained, but become liberated as they come to understand that the shadows on the wall do not make up reality at all. Consciousness of how knowledge is constructed and maintained increases the likelihood that reality will be seen as it is, rather than the mere shadows seen by the prisoners. As in *The Matrix* (Silver, Wachowski, & Wachowski, 1999), those who remain mindlessly plugged in to the system operate in a dreamlike reality that allows for manipulation and promotes the defense of a structure that serves interests other than liberation and social justice. To be conscious, on the other hand, is to develop what Freire (1970) calls *conscientiacao* or conscientization. Conscientization is a process through which students, as empowered subjects, acquire a deepening awareness of the contextual realities that shape their lives and begin to discover their own capacities to recreate them (Darder et al., 2009). Thus, rather than becoming victims to historical determinism, students come to realize the conditioning they receive in order to become liberated from it: to move toward becoming authors of their own lives. Without such critical consciousness, social justice efforts are impotent. Quite simply, we can't change what we do not see is changeable.

Conclusion

Critical pedagogy is offered as an alternative to status quo–reifying, technocratic, and reductionistic educational methods based on positivist assumptions of knowledge as described here and in Chapter One. Critical pedagogy has evolved out of the desire to promote democratic education, to critique static schooling practices, and to transform "conditions within society that functioned to thwart the democratic participation of all people" (Darder et al., 2009). The connection between critical pedagogy and social justice is clear. Like critical theory, critical pedagogy is concerned both with emancipatory educational methods and the ultimate liberation for all in which critical consciousness functions to sustain a free society. Critical pedagogy serves as a fundamental foundation for social justice education and action. Understanding the nature of knowledge as socially constructed, historically produced, economically influenced, mediated through hegemony, and reinforced through power is a complex journey, but necessary for developing an effective social justice practice. The professional behaviors congruent with such a journey include reflective praxis, ethical commitment, respect for the lived experience and knowledge of students, driving curiosity, ego-challenging awareness of the reality of our being unfinished, and an entrenched belief in the human capacity for transformation. Such transformation is best conceived through a metaphor of loving relationship forged through intimate dialogue, shared vision, and even moments of questioning our commitments. Just as important is the antidogmatic practice of persistently holding our own beliefs up to recursive scrutiny.

Some of the tales of oppression described earlier in this book and the dramatic inequalities that still exist in our democracy can lead many to cynicism or at least passive acceptance of the seemingly overwhelming forces that maintain oppression. Freire (2000) and others warn us of the dangers of neoliberal reactions and policies that accept the resigned logic informing contemporary culture today. Freire challenges us to battle the fatalistic tendencies birthed from a belief that cultural reality and social-historical evolution are unalterable. The critical perspective offered in this chapter, in contrast, provides a schema that educators can critique, engage, and hopefully employ. We believe that by doing so, by treating students as fully capable beings in all of their and our humanness, we create sites both in and outside of the classroom as spaces of student empowerment, cultural transformation, and social justice. Critical pedagogy, through its illumination of power, history, and political-economic contexts, as well as its unveiling of hegemony, technical rationalism, and ideology, promotes a form of critique, dialectical dialogue, resistance, and praxis necessary to effectively promote social justice in higher education.

5

Situating the Self

Barriers to and Strategies for Effective Social Justice Education

Faculty members commonly joke, "My students are getting younger and younger every year." Or a professor might describe some egregious student behavior and protest, "I would never have done that as a student." But these comments are often expressed as criticisms of the students rather than as a reflection of the instructor's own ignorance, discomfort, or vulnerability. Although we can poke fun at the growing age gap between ourselves and our students, we are much less likely to say, "I don't want to get up there and make a fool of myself—I have no idea how to relate to them."

—Therese Huston (2009, pp. 22–23)

One of the key principles in social justice education, related to the postpositivist epistemological perspective we've outlined, is that an educator cannot exist in a separate, objective space from those he or she seeks to educate. This chapter continues our shift from the conceptual foundations of social justice to negotiating the complexities of translating theory into practice. Educators must constantly navigate nuances related to balancing the intellectual and emotional issues raised in social justice practice. We explore barriers specific to engaging students in educational environments with social justice content. In addition, theoretical and practical strategies for negotiating these hurdles are identified and explored.

During office hours one afternoon, a student came to see me (Harrison) about his paper. In the course of our conversation, he told me about another professor who was "asking me to reflect about things I don't want to reflect on." While I tried to think of an appropriately professorial response, his eyes started to well up. Mine did, too, in an involuntary, physical reaction to another person's pain. I told him, as gently as possible, that when you work in a helping profession, you have to be reflective or you risk hurting the people you want to help. He considered this. Then he said, "I want to keep this compartmentalized. It was awful being gay where I grew up." Then he was crying for real. It took everything inside of me not to cry, too. The professorial and personal responses within me were at odds in that moment. Dr. Harrison wanted to ask him how he might balance the requirements of the assignment with his psychological needs. Laura wanted to hold him. Both felt incomplete and inadequate.

We ask a lot of students in social justice education classes and programs. Maybe it's a simple realization, but we don't often fully remember this until a student is either crying or frustrated in our offices, shaking us like we've probably jarred countless students as they try to wrestle with the academic and personal aspects of human diversity. We're professors, so we're technically only in charge of the academic realm. But we haven't found that to be a very effective approach if we really want students to engage on a deeper level with the realities of racism, sexism, heterosexism, and all the other -isms that could be added here. So how do educators strike a reasonable balance between dealing with their students' heads and hearts when it comes to the volatile issues any good multicultural class would address? How do we find a way to maintain professional boundaries without sterilizing the potentially dynamic classroom space? Is there a way to allow our students to challenge one another without hurting each other in that process?

Barriers

Let's face it; the student we described is not the kind of person most educators dread in social justice classes. So another important question to ask is: How ought we deal with ourselves and our students when they push our buttons? Not all students can express themselves as honestly and bravely as the young man who came into Laura's office that afternoon. Sometimes students say derogatory, accusatory, and ignorant things in social justice classes. While their presentation may vary wildly, their experience may be the same as the student described above. One key to reaching students in classes where we ask them to "reflect on things they don't want to reflect on" is to really see that student, even if he or she is buried deeply in the shell of someone acting out. No doubt this is a difficult proposition. This chapter does not promise a magic formula for developing what the great psychologist Carl Rogers (1961) called "unconditional positive regard" for every student with whom one interacts. It's a nice idea, but we argue it represents one of the fallacies that make the multicultural education enterprise tougher than it needs to be by setting an unrealistic outcome goal. Yet educators have to find ways to empathize with students in order to establish the trust necessary for them to take intellectual risks. Successful social justice education is a both-and proposition that relies heavily on the ability to hold seemingly contradictory ideas. It's a challenging prospect to model the content one strives to teach in a class without stepping on the myriad land mines that can derail the process. We will identify barriers to successful social justice education, which occur both in and outside of the classroom, and suggest strategies that do not necessarily avoid these barriers, but that might offer a path through them.

Mental Models Based on Dominant Narratives about Difference

Some of the problems that make social justice education classes less effective than they could be occur before either the professor or students set foot on campus. Studies show students hold negative perceptions of professors of color and women faculty as well as course content dedicated to issues of oppression (Tuitt, Hanna, Martinez, Salazar, & Griffin, 2009). Similarly, educators of color and women carry with them additional burdens such as more frequent attacks on their credibility, particularly when teaching social justice–oriented classes (Turner, Gonzalez, & Wood, 2008). As a result, both students and educators can enter the social justice educational space in a spirit of defensiveness. Goff, Steele, and Davies (2008), for example, found that whites tended to distance themselves from black conversation partners out of fear of being labeled racist. Similarly, members of target groups frequently report feeling pressured to speak on behalf of all people of color, women, and so on when diversity within these groups is not recognized. Acknowledgment that students and educators do not leave the unequal systems and biased assumptions that define the world simply because they entered a classroom or educational intervention seems a logical first step in addressing the challenges of social justice education.

Socialization against frank discussions of difference presents another challenge in the social justice–oriented classroom. Markus and Moya (2010) outline the ways in which U.S. popular culture discourages serious conversation about race out of concerns ranging from perceived politeness (for example, "I don't see color") to more ideologically driven desires to diminish the reality of its continued significance (for example, "we have a black president, so everything is okay now"). Students may be too sophisticated to make these exact statements, but their thinking is no doubt influenced by the dominant discourse about difference in our country.

When educators push against this notion by pointing out systemic inequalities, students may react out of genuine confusion as their minds reset to an intellectual default of sorts that signals to them that we live in a postracial, postfeminist world. Further, the rugged individualism that characterizes the positivist, Western paradigm exacerbates students' already wary view of systemic rather than individual explanations for inequality. Add their previous twelve-plus years in educational systems largely informed by this mental model and one can see fairly quickly why students might need some help adjusting to the kind of learning required in a social justice education curriculum. How students express this disorientation can range from silence to anger to questions and statements that offend both educators and fellow students. These are critical moments that have the potential to transform young minds and hearts or push them back into uncritical spaces of accepting the dominant discourse about difference.

Students are never blank slates, but they are even less so in the context of a social justice education course. Unlike a botany class, where they are likely to enter the room ready to believe what the professor has to say on the topic, students come into a social justice–oriented class with many preconceived notions about the subject matter and experiences as men, women, transgender people, white people, people of color, and so on. To complicate matters, they are unlikely to know most of the assumptions they hold because that is the nature of assumptions: they operate as default settings of which we are generally unaware. Assumptions are existentially different from positions; we know what we believe about affirmative action or gay marriage, for example. The assumption level, however, works at best semiconsciously, shaping our thoughts, feelings, beliefs, and positions, but in a covert way that feels to us like objective reality. Senge (1994) refers to this phenomenon as "mental models," the ways in which we come to understand the world that feel like "just the way things are," but which are actually constructed and therefore changeable. The idea that reality is objective is a concept explored more fully in Chapter One, but it is relevant here as an intellectual tool students must understand if they are to consider new knowledge on a topic they tend to think they know intuitively.

Teaching about mental models is an admittedly formidable task because it demands a level of intellectual and personal engagement not always asked of students. Unlike botany, where students generally do not need to unlearn a dominant discourse about plants, social justice education requires a highly challenging process of examining the very nature of how one thinks about what one knows. This is difficult intellectually; students rightly grapple with the discomfort of finding out that what they accepted as objective truth might not be so. Unlike the proverbial fish in water, the student also carries the added burden of the emotional fallout that accompanies disequilibrium. Students' mental models don't just come from popular culture; they are formed by parents, friends, and other people they know and love. Documented in both scholarly literature and popular culture, students often feel a sense of loss when they acquire new knowledge that puts them at odds with their families and communities. This very real tension provides good reason for students to resist information, even when they cannot put their finger on the precise source of their anxiety. When an educator essentially tells them they might be wrong, students understandably react in myriad ways, ranging from defensiveness to embarrassment to shutting down. Again, the difference in whether these moments inspire fresh thinking or raise hackles depends a lot on how they are both understood and addressed.

Students' Intellectual-Emotional Tensions in the Classroom

We've both experienced and heard anecdotes about many social justice–oriented classes and programs opening with deliberately provocative exercises like having students generate as many stereotypes as they can about particular groups or name their personal biases. While we can understand the impulse behind such techniques, we have also experienced the negative consequences of asking students to divulge too much too soon. Basic counseling and psychology theories posit rapport as an essential foundation for any sort of change work, which is clearly integral to social justice education. Ignoring the affective environment is perhaps the surest way to sabotage learning, particularly when the material is likely to elicit strong personal reactions. Methodical preparation and brilliant lecturing do not compensate for attending to the emotional experience of students, whose ability to learn is strongly correlated to how they feel in the classroom setting. Students consistently rate caring as the hallmark of excellent educators, above even knowledge or enthusiasm for the subject (Moore & Kuol, 2007).

When academic environments do not dismiss emotions entirely, they tend to deal with them as problems to be managed or controlled. It seems unlikely that educators, who are, after all, human beings, too, would consciously choose to pathologize feelings. Heron (1982) provided a plausible explanation, highlighting the ways in which the prevailing mental model of education emphasizes a control paradigm: "If a disease model or treatment model of working on feelings is adopted, then professional helpers of all kinds—from teachers to doctors—exempt themselves from personal work on feelings on the grounds that they are normal, not ill" (p. 36). Despite years of literature on the benefits of alternative pedagogies (explored in Chapter Four), the dominant narrative of education in our society parallels the disease model. In this paradigm, feelings are at best side effects to be minimized and at worst threats to the efficient process of knowledge transmission. This understanding persists, despite volumes of research demonstrating the connections between how students feel and what they are able to learn.

We're not suggesting turning classes into group therapy; in fact, we believe the intellectual realm is both an appropriate and effective starting point in an academic environment, understanding that the distinction between the cognitive and affective is largely artificial. Beginning from an intellectual framework accomplishes several important goals. First, it cues the students to understand that while they may have ideas and opinions about social justice, they are in an academic setting where there is a knowledge base they must access to inform their thinking as it evolves. Second, beginning in the conceptual realm feels "normal" for students; they understand what it means to be in a class and can leverage this sense of familiarity as the boundary needed when they are asked to explore unchartered terrain. Finally, focusing on the academic aspects of social justice can have a democratizing effect, providing a common language in which to ground divergent experiences. This allows for a bridge between the intellectual and emotional, experiences that can never be fully divorced, but which can be leveraged through emphasis and deemphasis at certain points.

For example, I (Harrison) start with mental models when I teach almost any class, but particularly those with strong social justice content. After explaining the concept, I transition into my own experience of seeing a mental model I hold. I intentionally choose a fairly benign one, such as my experience trying to drive in New Zealand. I use this story to show students how I could not understand that I drove on the right until I tried to drive on the left. I then move into a slightly more relevant example, which occurred when I moved to California and began noticing how late everyone was to meetings, classes, and appointments more generally. As a punctual Midwesterner, this annoyed me and I generalized my early experiences to form a mental model of all Californians as chronically tardy. Whenever someone was on time to a meeting, I assumed that person was not a native Californian, and this turned out to be true most of the time. It was not true all of the time, but my mind did what minds do and began to treat evidence that contradicted my mental model as outliers. At this point, I usually take a side trip into Kahneman's (2011) excellent work on how and why brains do this, emphasizing that it's not an entirely bad thing. Brains create patterned understandings of things so that we don't have to relearn, for example, how to turn off our alarm clocks, make coffee, and brush our teeth every morning. These are good functions of mental models. Unfortunately, the same mechanisms that produce these positive results also create biases like the one that I formed about Californians; these assumptions are so powerful that they feel like objective reality, not a position one consciously holds on a matter. Because the mind preempts potentially oppositional evidence, the very nature of what we're even able to see is reconstituted into our preconceived notion of what we're primed to see. I was able to see Californians as universally late because my mind erased the ones who were on time before I could even process them as evidence contrary to my mental model.

Starting with a mental model about Californians plays well, particularly now that I'm teaching in the Midwest. It actually worked all right in California, too, where students didn't mind being characterized as tardy, often providing their own stories that supported my mental model. When this happened, I used it to introduce the topic of language as reifying; that is, language that both creates and reflects reality. I could demonstrate in real time how we were forming a collective mental model as a class about the nature of Californians and their relationship to time by emphasizing certain aspects of one another's stories and deemphasizing others. Students could see in that moment how this process of reinforcing our shared assumptions strengthened them, causing us to make increasingly bold statements that evolved into a great example of groupthink. Eventually, we would reach the point of outlandishness and students could start making connections about how this process might play out with truly marginalized groups.

Part of the reason this exercise works, we think, is that everyone has experienced something like having to drive on the other side of the road or feeling another kind of real or perceived shift in norms. Having a common experience from which to begin allows students and professors alike the freedom to not, for example, expect other people in the room to automatically "get it" because they are women, people of color, and so on. Further, appropriate self-disclosure about a prejudicial perspective allows the professor to model the kind of sharing he or she aims to see in students. In other words, telling stories that one accepts as his or her own, that demonstrate some intellectual risk taking, and that raise questions in an exploratory fashion rather than making blanket statements demonstrates important aspects of social justice discourse.

Of course, when you teach this way, you have to be prepared for a student to say something like this, which happened to me (Harrison) in one of my very first social justice education programs:

> I really get what you're saying. I was raised in a very liberal household where my parents and siblings were moral relativists about everything. Being from San Francisco, I think this is probably a common experience. I sort of blindly accepted that there were no real rights or wrongs until I found Jesus in my life and started to see the fallacy of that way of thinking. I began to understand for myself that a lot of what goes wrong in our world comes from people thinking anything goes. I don't consider myself prejudiced, but I did vote for Prop 8 [the anti-same-sex marriage ballot initiative in California] because I finally found the courage to decide for myself that I really do believe marriage should be between one man and one woman.

A lot happened for me as a professor and as a human being in that moment. My eyes immediately and involuntarily shifted to the two openly LGBT students in the room, one of whom looked like she was ready to fight while the other clearly disassociated into her iPhone. The former launched into an intellectualized but also personal attack on the Christian student, while the rest of the group either shifted uncomfortably in their seats or shot hands into the air to line up behind one or the other of the students, who were pretty close to yelling at one another. I felt the fight-or-flight sensation that tends to accompany these kinds of situations, but then reminded myself that an actual lion was not coming at me and that I therefore had some time and space to respond thoughtfully, rather than reacting in a knee-jerk fashion. On the human level, I was surprised and hurt by the Christian student, whom I had always liked and from whom I felt a great deal of respect. I also wanted to defend the lesbian student, with whom I felt both solidarity as "my people" and absolute agreement in what she was now saying about the ways in which real Christianity had been coopted. And, to be honest, it was a challenge not to let my little classroom become the stage on which the big drama of this issue could play out differently with me as the director. While I would certainly not grade the Christian student differently, I could, and it would be difficult to imagine the knowledge of that not affecting both of our behavior in the moment. I have no way of knowing this, but she could very easily have been holding back more intense comments based on the power dynamic in the room. And my position as the issuer rather than the recipient of grades doubtlessly informed my ability not to feel threatened by her. Had she been grading me (or voting on my tenure), her heterosexual privilege may have had more consequence in my life. But it was not about me in that moment; it was about protecting a process in which we had to find a way to both take risks and maintain safety, if not comfort. By focusing on the academic process and not my personal-political stance, I was able to raise important questions without being dogmatic. I was also able to challenge the students with whom I agreed to use appropriate discussion norms and avoid personal attacks. Educators will experience varying levels of cognitive understanding and fluctuating emotional connections to the material, but we all have in common a requirement to maintain a respectful process where learning can occur.

Power as Simultaneously Exercised and Critiqued

Part of the challenge in leading a social justice–oriented class is the often ambivalent relationship educators have with power. On the one hand, the very nature of social justice education necessitates a critique of power as it exposes the hierarchies that lead to dominance and subordination in society. It would be an abdication of responsibility to let students leave a course on social justice without understanding how the historical and contemporary misuses of power lead to systemic inequality. Whatever else might be included in a social justice curriculum, this concept is generally understood as key. Logically, then, it tends to occur to social justice educators that a hierarchical, top-down approach to the class might present a contradiction to the material being presented in such a course.

There are many benefits to modeling the empowerment of students in the context of teaching a critique of power in the context of social justice education. Sharing power with students makes us smarter as educators by helping us avoid problematic and inaccurate diagnoses of conflicts that occur in the classroom. Palmer (2007) provides a cautionary tale about the consequences of a top-down approach to education:

> We allow our "treatment mode" to be shaped by the thoughtless stereotypes of students that float freely in faculty culture. The dominant diagnosis, to put it bluntly, is that our "patients" are brain-dead. Small wonder, then, that the dominant treatment is to drip data bits into our students' veins, wheeling their comatose forms from one information source to the next until the prescribed course of treatment is complete.... This caricature highlights a truth: our assumption that students are brain-dead leads to pedagogies that deaden their brains [pp. 710–716].

Respecting students as colearners can inoculate educators against the too common rhetoric of students as slackers who need to be controlled. While few educators would probably consciously characterize students in this manner, Palmer's (2007) point about the dominant discourse rings true. This negative generalization not only leads to poor diagnoses of the social justice classroom's challenges but also relieves the educator of responsibility for creating and implementing an educational environment that sets students up for success.

It is at this point of holding the process that educators must balance empowering students with not relinquishing their power as facilitators. While respecting students as equal human beings yields positive results, abandoning one's role as a leader can lead to significant problems. The social justice educator has to walk a fine line between empowering students and holding a process that creates the trust necessary to do the hard work of challenging assumptions. Sometimes this means acknowledging that the classroom is not an entirely democratic space. In most cases, for example, faculty create the syllabus, set the behavioral expectations, and issue grades, even if they do these things with flexibility and/or student input. Further, there are situations in which the responsible course of action is for educators to exercise their authority. I recall an instance in which three students were consistently disruptive in a class despite my efforts to talk to them and find out what I could do to reach them. One day, I made the decision to throw them out of class because their behavior had reached the point where it was impeding other students' right to learn. My class was shocked, especially given the social justice content of the class. It was uncomfortable, but I used it as an example to talk about my own ambivalence accessing power in that moment. I took the time to explain my thinking and decision-making process, which two of the three students whom I dismissed later said they appreciated.

Another benefit of owning one's power is that it encourages students to understand that there is a knowledge base they are expected to learn. While respecting students' feelings is important, students too often mistake the idea of subjective realities with the notion that social justice education is all a matter of opinion. Exercising authority in the best sense of the word—as an extension of authorship—helps students distinguish between political views and academic material. In a discussion of her research and experience as a social justice educator, W. Randolph explains this process well:

> My role is to walk students through the cognitive disso-
> nance that happens when I push up against the master
> narrative. I expect resistance, I understand it, I am com-
> fortable with their silences, and I address these things
> through bringing them back to the data [Randolph,
> personal communication, March 2, 2012].

Simultaneously empowering students while maintaining the positive aspects of authority poses many challenges, but offers substantive benefits. Students appreciate both these outcomes achieved by honest communication about educators' thinking as they negotiate the many nuances involved with negotiating power in the social justice classroom.

Educators' Intellectual-Emotional Tensions in the Classroom

At first glance, it appears to be a mystery why so much of what goes on in the classroom mirrors Palmer's (2007) caricature of educators treating students like comatose patients. No one aspires to teach like this, so why does it happen? Palmer (2007) presents stereo-typing of students as one answer, but what is the root of the stereotyping? Again, no one would strive to conceptualize students negatively and, if he or she did, why would a person want to teach people of whom they thought so little? The more plausible explanation is not that we really think so little of students, but that we sometimes refuse to face our own fears. Park (2011) captured the experience with impressive concision and authenticity:

> Inviting students to coconstruct meaning on issues of
> race is a somewhat scary and risky concept to me as a fac-
> ulty member of color. It is tempting for me to not want
> to give students space to grapple, sometimes awkwardly,
> with issues that are so personal to me [pp. 233–234].

It's tempting and, frankly, easier to blame the students than to be honest about our own anxieties about teaching material that is personally meaningful and potentially charged. Students sometimes hurt us in their grappling and we're not supposed to be hurt because we're told feelings have no place in academia. So we get stuck and need to question the prevailing thinking about the role of emotions in intellectual environments or we wind up with no healthy outlet for what happens to us in these spaces. And, without a positive place to put these experiences, it becomes very easy to inadvertently take them out on the students.

At the other extreme of projecting onto the students is the sometimes crushing need for approval many of us face, especially teaching material with which we tend to feel a personal connection. It can be overwhelming to teach about the big issues that affect our lives on a daily basis, especially since the emotional aspect cannot truly be ignored. We need permission for it to be enough that our students grasp the material and treat both each other and us with respect, not necessarily approval. Bell, Washington, Weinstein, and Love (2003) articulate this distinction well:

> In the social justice classroom we intentionally create tension to disrupt complacent and unexamined attitudes about social life. These very conditions can cause students to dislike or feel hostile toward us at various points in the course. Confronting oppression invariably involves a range of feelings from anxiety, confusion, anger, and sadness to exhilaration and joy. We need to remind ourselves that as much as we crave approval from our students, a sense of well-being and long-term learning are not necessarily synonymous. A better indication of our effectiveness might be whether students leave with more questions than they came in with, wanting to know more and questioning core assumptions in their own socialization [p. 472].

It is not our students' job to validate our experiences, nor is this a realistic expectation of them, particularly in classes where they need the freedom and space to wrestle with difficult material. Social justice educators need not feel bad for wanting to be liked; in fact, a frank acknowledgment of this human quality is probably the only way to ensure it doesn't get in the way of the students' learning. Proactively seeking outlets to discharge these anxieties with one's support system can go a long way in allowing ourselves to center the students' needs rather than our own in the social justice classroom. Conversely, pretending students never push our buttons or hurt us in their grappling can create a defensiveness in us that gets in the way of the very behaviors we would want to model. If educators deny their own struggles, it is unlikely students will take the personal and intellectual risks necessary to engage challenging social justice material with the depth needed to learn in any meaningful way.

Strategies

We've been called too liberal, too conservative, and a host of other things by students struggling to deal with the incredibly difficult task of engaging in civil discourse. Much like the institutionalized racism, sexism, and other -isms that are not left at the door when students and faculty walk into a social justice class, civil discourse is not something that just happens by entering a particular space. Examples of uncivil discourse abound in our society; faculty cannot assume students have the tools to engage in the intellectually challenging, potentially painful conversations that one can expect to arise in any class focused on social justice issues. It is therefore crucial that educators anticipate the host of challenges that one might expect in a situation where students are asked to engage with topics they have been explicitly socialized to avoid. In the situation with the Christian student, it was easy to feel like my (Harrison's) only options were correcting what I do believe were faulty assumptions on her part or avoiding the issue out of a vague notion that all viewpoints are acceptable. Especially in the heat of the moment, it can be difficult to access some of the other responses that might move the dialogue forward.

Immediacy

The first strategy that can ameliorate situations like these is immediacy. Immediacy is the quality of staying present. A deceptively simple concept, immediacy allows people to respond to the unique nuances of what is happening in a specific moment. For example, the gay-Christian issue has been played so many times in the media that it is difficult to not have knee-jerk reactions based on generalized caricatures rather than responses to how it is playing out with *these* unique people in *this* particular context. Without immediacy, the tendency is to *react* rather than *respond*, which can create a vicious circle. For example, if I (Harrison) had reacted out of fear by squelching the discussion, I would have modeled to the class that some conversations are too scary to have and/or that I distrusted their ability to engage in difficult dialogues. Or, if I had told the Christian student she was wrong, I very likely would have reinforced a mental model about all professors having a liberal bias and/or that only some ideas were welcome in my class.

Both of these reactions present common temptations based on either painful past experiences or a projected future of flared tempers or possible chaos. By employing immediacy, educators and students can stay in the present, where the information is richer and therefore the possibilities are wider. For example, I had prior knowledge of these students and could reasonably predict they were not actually going to fight or fall apart in class. I also knew that both of them liked to try out new ideas, which I endorsed actively in my classes. I had to balance my knowledge of them with active attention to what they were saying so that I could respond in a way that was thoughtful and appropriate to this unique situation. Otherwise, I might have imposed prescribed solutions as a template of sorts, missing the educational opportunity out of fear based on societal tropes of this issue. By staying in the moment with them, my choices for responding widened beyond general statements to more honest observations like, "I would not have imagined the application of the concept in this way, but am glad to see your thought process as you struggle to make it your own." Questions also emerge when we're really present in a moment, often proving more helpful than statements. We can ask questions like, "What role does the media play in constructing heterosexual marriage as a default and same-sex marriage as an issue?" This kind of question helps students connect their opinions to underlying assumptions about how issues are framed, reemphasizing the knowledge base critical to meaningful, effective social justice education. Immediacy allows educators and students to stay present with one another as they cocreate the best path through the unique labyrinth in which they find themselves.

Perhaps most important, immediacy increases the likelihood of a better diagnosis. In the aforementioned case, it would have been easy to react to the loudest players, attending to their needs without realizing the student on her iPhone actually needed some focus. Immediacy slows down what can feel like a runaway train situation by creating heightened focus on what is really happening in a moment. As a result, it becomes easier to see how what appears to be the obvious issue on the surface might not actually warrant the most attention. Staying present allows educators to read and respond more effectively to the complicated dynamics that occur in the complex space of the social justice classroom.

Appropriate Self-Disclosure

Appropriate self-disclosure is what makes immediacy possible. Educators who attempt to remove themselves entirely from the learning process risk creating classroom experiences that are boring and stilted. Students perform what they see modeled; a professor who refuses to acknowledge her or his own emotional state is unlikely to inspire students to make this kind of leap. Further, refusal to engage personally makes real-time responding almost impossible because being present requires going off the script. Deviating from a prescribed plan necessitates an openness and vulnerability on the educator's part, trusting the process enough to walk willingly into some discomfort to achieve a greater good than could be garnered through a control paradigm.

While immediacy requires some self-disclosure, it must be appropriate to be effective. This is an admittedly delicate equilibrium, especially considering the shifting and ideological nature of what is appropriate. Mortiboys (2012) offers insightful guideposts for negotiating this balance:

> [To] suppress your feelings, to deny their importance or just pretend they are not there—this can lead to more stress for you and poor relationships with others if you are withholding your feelings for them. In doing this, you are not showing respect for yourself and it makes it almost impossible for you to accept others who do express their feelings. The other extreme is to blurt it all out in every detail and let everybody know how you are feeling all of the time, which is overwhelming for the recipient, indulgent on your part and unprofessional [p. 115].

This strategy can look relatively simple as words on a page, but anyone who has taught a class with charged content knows what a daunting task it can actually be to hold this paradox of being present and holding back. For us, what drives this process is students' best interest. Before we share what we're thinking or how we're feeling, we try to ask ourselves what our motivations are for communicating it. If it's about making us feel better, being right, or fixing something, we try to refrain because those things are not our job in that moment. If we think our thoughts or feelings will help a student understand something on a deeper level, we both generally take the risk. In both our experiences as well as the volumes of developmental literature on traditional-age college students, authenticity is something on which they place a high premium, even if they disagree with a point. We've found students appreciate it when we can express what's going on for us in a moment with words like, "I'm struggling right now because I value your application of the theory and agree with your right to believe as you do while really disagreeing with what you said." When we can model openness, candor about struggle, and staying present despite discomfort, they see that they, too, have more options than they think for engaging the admittedly rocky emotional terrain that characterizes the social justice classroom.

Moving Past "Getting It" to "Being in It"

Conflict plays a central role in the social justice classroom. This is a challenging prospect in a culture where conflict is generally perceived as a negative thing to be avoided. One of the first tasks in social justice education is to unpack this phenomenon to show how conflict avoidance serves the status quo by framing those who challenge it as argumentative or rude. This can be useful in demonstrating how a custom that presents as an ideologically neutral practice of being polite actually assists those in power by making it untenable to challenge or question their dominance. Helping students understand the vital role of conflict in stimulating social change is an important learning outcome in social justice education.

Equally important to articulating conflict's role in promoting equity is teaching students how to negotiate conflict. Their (and our) first reaction to tension is often fight or flight, both of which perpetuate what Stone, Patton, and Heen (2000) call win-lose scenarios. When conflicts are framed in the language of positions, the result is that someone has to win and someone has to lose. Stone et al. (2000) suggest story as an alternative to position in conceptualizing conflict. Positions tend to be reductive and dichotomous; I am "pro-choice" or "pro-life" or "for" or "against" capital punishment, as examples. Stories, on the other hand, provide a more detailed, nuanced, personal, and complete picture of where a person may be coming from. Stories are also more fluid; we may indeed disagree on abortion or the death penalty, but there may be broader concepts like freedom and justice that resonate with one another, even if they lead us to different conclusions about an issue. Similarly, stories allow us to see the path that led us to believe as we do. Again, we may not like where the other person lands, but we understand more clearly how he or she got there.

The opposite of this approach is what we have heard too often referred to as the "getting it" approach to social justice education. In this paradigm, educators characterize students as either "getting it" or "not getting it," the "it" serving as shorthand for "what I believe to be true." Students sometimes rightly accuse educators of trying to indoctrinate them politically; we believe we sometimes deny and dismiss these claims too easily when they in fact ring true in some cases. The line between the content to be covered and the political conclusions one might draw based on that content is admittedly blurry. But that is not an excuse to marginalize students with sincere intellectual disagreements about a topic as "not getting it." Mundell (2011) articulated this distinction well:

> I have also encountered students who get turned off to discussing matters of race because educators have assumed they did not understand the subtle and complex ways racial prejudices continue in our society. Many students today do recognize the existence of racism and its ongoing impact, but they genuinely disagree with the necessity of continuing to discuss it. In the eyes of these individuals, they get that institutionalized racism still exists—but also believe that it is slowly but surely fading away. And if slavery stands as our country's original sin (as our president has suggested), these students believe it is a fair question to ask when we will know that redemption has been achieved [p. 241].

Not only is the "getting it" paradigm disrespectful to students, but it creates undue pressure on social justice educators as well. If we understood our jobs as convincing students to vote like we do or refrain from what we feel is sexist or racist thinking, we would be paralyzed by the enormity of that task. As it is, we believe our role is to introduce students to concepts like hegemony and master narrative so they have the tools they need to think through social justice issues individually and collectively. We want them to think critically and develop informed perspectives on these vital topics so they become more thoughtful, humane citizens. As human beings, we of course have our ideas about what that looks like and in some ways hope their thoughts and feelings will align with ours. And if we were working as lobbyists or at a think tank, our jobs would be to push an agenda. As it is, our job is to give students the intellectual tools to navigate social justice issues in all their complexity. This distinction in how we conceptualize our work as social justice educators allows us to develop learning outcomes that are both more tenable and empathic.

Connection, Trust, and Vulnerability

While social justice–themed courses and programs present some unique challenges, success in teaching them rests on the same qualities that research suggests creates successful learning environments for students in any class. The first quality that creates positive outcomes is connection. Connection is what students usually mean when they praise a class as "relevant" or criticize it as "random." If students sense a disconnect between the learning material and what matters to them in their own lives, they are unlikely to take ownership for their own education in a class. Simply asking students what is important to them and framing the material in the context of some of their responses goes a long way in helping apply the course content in ways that are meaningful for them. Demonstrating respect by asking students what is important to them also serves to build the rapport necessary for the hard work of engaging the challenging material that constitutes social justice curricula.

Connecting with students requires trust in their capacity as learners. In Bain's (2004) remarkable study of the best college professors, trust emerged as a consistent theme that distinguished excellent teaching. Trust can seem like an ethereal concept, but behaviors resulting from a trusting versus a distrusting attitude accounted for measurable differences between professors who were highly effective and those who weren't. For example, educators who approached students from a spirit of trust owned responsibility for the learning environment and, "believed students wanted to learn, and they assumed, until proven otherwise, that they could learn. That attitude found reflection in scores of small and large practices. It led to high expectations and to the habit of looking inward for any problems rather than blaming some alleged student deficiency" (p. 140). Bain (2004) pointed out that this finding applied whether educators worked in highly selective or open admissions colleges, as well as across demographic differences. He acknowledged that even excellent faculty can have a bad day and sometimes find students frustrating, a point worth reiterating. The difference, however, seems to lie in a deeper attitude or mental model from which educators approach students, either as negative and lacking or positive and full of potential.

When faculty trust students, they are also more likely to share their own intellectual journeys, including struggles that often serve as the foundation for students to feel safe enough to admit their weaknesses and get the help they need. Trusting students necessitates a willingness to be vulnerable, to let ourselves be seen by students so that they might let themselves be seen by us. When students let themselves be seen, they take intellectual risks, try out ideas, and connect in ways that help them move past the paralysis that can happen in classrooms where people are posturing or acting out of defensiveness. Brown (2010) conducted cutting-edge research on shame and vulnerability and concluded: "When we don't give ourselves permission to be free, we rarely tolerate that freedom in others. We put them down, make fun of them, ridicule their behaviors, and sometimes shame them. We can do this intentionally or unconsciously" (p. 123).

For better or worse, it seems our only option in not replicating the same systems we seek to dismantle in the social justice classroom is to model the trust we ask of our students in these spaces. Inherent to trust is vulnerability; taking risks and truly trying on new mental models are risky endeavors that make people feel uncomfortable and uncertain. Someone has to go first.

Conclusion

While good teaching in social justice education classes ultimately requires the same qualities as good teaching in any other class, material that confronts dominant discourses presents unique challenges in these learning environments. When educators confront students' mental models, defensiveness, anger, and pain sometimes result. Navigating these reactions successfully necessitates balancing an acknowledgment of affect with appropriate boundaries. Perhaps the first step is simply to anticipate these realities so that one is not blindsided by them.

Students need spaces to think out loud, to try out new ideas, and wrestle with concepts without being labeled sexist or racist in response to an honest exploration. They may in fact be sexist or racist, as we all are growing up in societies that remain unequal in a variety of ways. Yet understanding students as fundamentally good and approaching them with a spirit of trust seem to be the only ways out of the adversarial relationships that breed apathy and worse in any classroom. Students are keen observers. If educators' actions do not align with the course material regarding concepts like respect and being open minded, students will generally not engage with the course content. In our many years of teaching, we're increasingly convinced that the "how" is even more important than the "what" in education, particularly social justice–oriented courses. Students can Google much of what we tell them; what they need from us are living representations of balancing conviction with respect for other viewpoints, demonstrations of civil discourse, and that foundational rapport from which they feel empowered to try on new mental models.

We've read Tatum's (1997) groundbreaking book *Why Are All the Black Kids Sitting Together in the Cafeteria?* and are inspired by her bravery both in writing it and particularly in selecting the title. The title reflects the author's choice to point out a phenomenon that we've been socialized to pretend we don't notice. Through her willingness to make an observation, she gives the reader permission to unpack and understand this phenomenon in a deeper way. Toward the conclusion, she communicates well the attitude needed for effective social justice education:

> In nearly twenty years of teaching and leading workshops about racism, I have made many mistakes. I have found that a sincere apology and a genuine desire to learn from one's mistakes are usually rewarded with forgiveness. If we wait for perfection, we will never break the silence. The cycle of racism will continue uninterrupted [p. 281].

Forgiveness and tolerance for imperfection in our students and ourselves continue to be the keys to negotiating the many layers of nuance that make the social justice classroom a challenging but potentially richly rewarding site for effecting change.

6

Media Literacy

The media's the most powerful entity on earth. They have the power to make the innocent guilty and to make the guilty innocent and that's power. Because they control the minds of the masses.

—Malcolm X *(Handler, 1992)*

Similar to the way history textbooks as discussed in Chapter Three can skew reality in a way that favors those in power, media operate to sell a particular version of truth. Advertisements, movies, news reporting, and other forms of media sell a subjective perspective reflecting the political leanings of those funding its distribution. Often under the guise of neutrality and objectivity, various forms of media increasingly appear to use partial truths and misleading statements to sell voters and consumers. The problem is so pervasive that a number of reputable web sites like FactCheck.org and Politifact.com have emerged to critically examine media and political candidate claims. Unless we develop critical consumer skills, we risk being controlled by myths, partial truths, and lies that inhibit social justice.

I (Harrison) remember one of my first experiences studying media's role in perpetuating systemic inequality. I was in a women's studies class and the professor asked us to engage in the well-worn exercise of scouring advertisements for sexism. I picked up a few magazines and immediately chose pictures featuring women in domestic roles, smiling happily while serving their presumed husbands and children dinner. The woman was almost always standing while the husband and children sat comfortably waiting for her to feed them. This pretty much represented my feminist nightmare scenario at the time and, I assumed, everyone else's.

I was surprised in class the following week that nearly all the other students brought beer ads to the class. I must have flipped past several of those without it once occurring to me that they were sexist. I was convinced by the ones featuring bikini-clad women offering beer to fully dressed businessmen because those represented a variation on the servitude theme I'd found in the ads I selected. But the ones where men and women were more or less equally naked and enjoying drinking together seemed okay to me. I didn't understand how or why nudity was inherently oppressive. Yes, the people featured in the ads met the mainstream metrics of beauty, but that was as true for the men as the women. I could accept their ads as examples of fat oppression or ageism or ableism, but they didn't seem sexist to me and I made the mistake of saying so, resulting in a poorly facilitated debate about objectification. In addition to my confusion about my classmates' ad choices, I fielded several semiaggressive questions about why I assumed cooking and child care were sexist, thereby contributing to society's devaluing of anything traditionally feminine. I understood the question, but my answer was simply, "Because I don't want to feel pressured to cook and have babies just because I'm a woman. But I do want to drink beer. And wear makeup. So I don't understand your ad choices." The professor said something about how we were all right because we were all entitled to our lenses and we moved on, but I remained confused.

I finished my women's studies degree mostly due to what I learned in other classes, but that class almost finished my women's studies career because I walked away from it thinking too much of the material was completely arbitrary. How could any of our ads be sexist or not simply because we were women and could choose to make that judgment based on our personal preferences? What did it matter, anyway, when there were so many more pressing social justice concerns in the world compared to how we felt about beer ads? Were the real issues like domestic violence and rape so thoroughly solved that possibly sexist ads were the only problems left to tackle in women's studies classes?

When these kinds of questions are left unresolved in students' minds, they can easily minimize post–Women's Movement, post–Civil Rights era social justice issues. Undoubtedly, the professor asked the students to participate in the exercise to show how media constructions of women contribute to a culture that continues to tolerate serious social injustices like rape and domestic violence. I'm sure she did explain this and it's possible I either didn't buy it or felt lost in my own confusion about the disparity between what the other students and I deemed to be sexist. It's also possible that the other students and I (and maybe even the professor) lacked the media literacy skills required to tackle such an assignment critically so that, while our interpretations might still differ, they would feel less arbitrary. This chapter argues for the centrality of media literacy in any social justice curriculum and presents key media literacy concepts students must grasp in order to understand media's role in systemic inequality.

The problem in the aforementioned scenario and in many social justice classrooms is that students and professors alike get stuck on the "what offends me" genre. This is unhelpful because of human variation; we'll never all be offended by the same things. Hart (2002), for example, wrote an interesting piece in the *Chronicle of Higher Education* detailing her and her colleagues' secret enjoyment of the politically incorrect television program *South Park*. Some people enjoy the show as brilliant satire, some like the show without understanding the satire, and some find its characters' frequent derogatory comments and/or bathroom humor offensive and juvenile regardless of satire. Thoughtful examination of how media reflects and creates social injustice requires moving past personal taste, which tends to get people stuck in a "what I like or don't like" conversation, rather than focusing on teaching students the critical thinking skills necessary to become informed media consumers.

Critical Thinking

Another reason the "what offends me" approach to media falls short is that it fails to explain more nuanced points about why a particular text is problematic. In "Everyday Pornography," for example, Caputi (2003) draws an important distinction between examining pornography from a moralistic framework about nudity and a feminist critique of the ideology that is often presented in this genre. She provides powerful examples of the ways in which pornography both reflects and creates male domination and female subordination through choices about how bodies are positioned, words used in captions ("Kick me," being two of the more memorable), and a host of other production choices. Feminists debate whether pornography is inherently oppressive, even in cases depicting women in servile roles which some reclaim as not necessarily demeaning in the context of some women's sexual preferences. This specific debate is beyond the scope of this chapter, but the point here is that no one is born knowing how to unmask the seemingly objective ways in which stories ranging from sexuality to politics to consumer products are told. Consequently, we need tools to be able to ask the critical questions necessary to become savvy consumers in the increasingly media-saturated world that informs our thinking every day.

Objectivity

The foundational critical thinking skill in media literacy is the ability to critique positivist notions of objectivity. Media stories and images are typically presented from an omniscient point of view, leaving readers with the impression that texts accurately reflect objective reality. This is particularly true in news media, which position themselves as "reporting," rather than "constructing" stories. The process by which choices about what to cover, which facts to emphasize, and, perhaps most important, what to omit remain hidden from the reader's vision. As a result, the reader feels like he or she is simply receiving factual information about an issue when the reality is that the final product has resulted from a series of calculated decisions influenced by reporters, writers, editors, and advertisers. This phenomenon is not necessarily wrong or problematic; all stories contain a point of view that shapes the content. The difference is that readers tend to experience the author's voice when reading a literary work; they understand that Shakespeare and Jackie Collins will present a love story differently based on several layers of identity, context, and quality. News stories, however, obscure these layers, creating a situation in which less informed readers fail to account for how these complex layers influence how an issue or topic is portrayed.

An example that illustrates this point occurred on the television news program *Democracy Now* in April 2012. In an interview about the student loan crisis, David Harvey, professor of anthropology at the Graduate Center of the City University of New York, proposed the idea of companies paying for higher education. He pointed out the ways in which universities have been coopted as training centers for industry's needs, leading him to argue that workers should not have to pay for their own training. Whether one agrees with Harvey's argument, the interview demonstrated the ways in which mainstream news outlets have framed this issue around certain assumptions that appear to be objective truths. The *Democracy Now* interview was the only place we observed the purpose of higher education and whose interests it serves as part of the coverage of the student loan crisis. Other news outlets used personal savings and university budget processes as starting points for addressing the issue. There is nothing wrong with these points; fiscal responsibility on the part of both students and universities no doubt plays a role in the student loan crisis. But these factors are just part of the incomplete, often distorted narrative that is written about higher education without the deeper context needed to understand the full story. In Chapter Four we discussed a "critical" approach that demands that we consider the contextual questions of whose interests are served, what economic benefits are obscured, and other dialectical inquiries that begin to unmask the connections between objective knowledge and underlying subjective norms, values, and standards.

Democracy Now is part of what one might consider "alternative media," meaning its coverage is filtered through a progressive lens. It could be argued that coverage on this show is biased, and we think that would be a true statement. The crucial point here, however, is that this statement is no more true of news outlets that admit their point of view than those that do not. For example, in much the same way that *Democracy Now* owns its progressive lens, the *National Review* expresses its conservative viewpoint. These news sources provide useful information to their audiences in ways that contrast with organizations like Fox News, which claim to offer "fair and balanced" coverage, but fail to deliver it. It is important to distinguish acknowledgement of bias from standards of credibility; people tend to conflate these two related but distinct points. Claims of objectivity do not equal credibility; in fact, more often than not they reflect a shallow understanding of an issue. There is no way to be objective about any important issue; positions on abortion or the death penalty, for instance, result from complex assumptions about human nature, freedom, which lives matter more, and a host of other values toward which we have been both consciously and unconsciously socialized. In addition, our preconceived views on these topics cause us to emphasize some information while deemphasizing other points when presented with news stories that support or contradict our paradigms. Moreover, the process by which something even becomes a named issue is less objective than it might seem. Gay marriage provides an effective example of this point. One would not expect to see a news story about heterosexual marriage, which appears to be simply normal, but which in fact privileges one way of living over another. Similarly, marriage itself is rarely critiqued; it is generally taken as a given that people would want to participate in this institution despite its checkered history as an economic arrangement having very little to do with love or affection. Again, the point here is not that marriage generally and gay marriage specifically are negative things, only that news stories covering them operate on a set of assumptions that present as objectivity, but actually prevent a more complete understanding of the issue.

Hence, media literacy requires disavowing credibility from claims of objectivity when evaluating a news story. Similarly, it is important not to conflate credibility with a "moderate" position, because moderation is a shifting target based on a belief in objectivity. A moderate view on the Israel-Palestine conflict, for instance, is not the same anywhere in the world. No news outlet can cover this issue and claim an unbiased, moderate position. There are, however, more credible ways of telling the story than others. The provision of deep history and context, multiple points of view, and sources not controlled by corporate or government interests are some variables to consider when assessing a news outlet's credibility. Objectivity, however, fails to stand up as a metric because media do not exist outside of the structurally unequal and complex world we all inhabit.

Ideology

Objectivity proves difficult to unpack because it presents as "just the way things are"—as a baseline normalcy that people take for granted. Ideology is a concept useful as a tool for exposing the ways in which seeming objectivity actually masks a point of view. Paul and Elder (2006) present a useful example of the ways objectivity becomes more of a shifting target than it may appear: "The media will focus on what their readers personally care about. Thus, even if their readers are irrational in some belief (for example, they harbor some irrational hate), the media nevertheless will treat that hatred as rational. Hence, when slavery was commonly accepted in the United States, the media presented slavery as 'natural.' When the country became divided on the issue, the media followed suit (each paper presenting as right what its readers believed to be right)" (p. 253). This example illustrates how dominant narratives constructed by those in power dictate how an issue is framed. A "middle-ground" position on slavery in the United States fluctuated as mental models about white supremacy shifted, landing in a contemporary understanding of no middle ground on this topic. This may appear obvious, but it has only become so from our contemporary vantage point.

What makes Paul and Elder's (2006) point so important is their use of the word *natural*. Words like *natural* and *normal* often conceal ideology that operates at the subterranean level in media presenting as objective. *Unnatural* and *abnormal* function in a comparable fashion, using pathology to uphold an ideological position. Jackson (2008) provides a good example of this phenomenon, explaining how nineteenth-century medical professionals diagnosed runaway slaves with a "mental disorder" referred to as "drapetomania." So at one time in our American history, slavery was natural, and attempts to escape slavery were abnormal. This is a more nuanced point than simple acknowledgment that the United States once endorsed slavery, then abolished it. What matters here is that the seemingly fixed categories of "natural" and "normal" did not stand up to what Martin Luther King Jr. referred to as the arc of the moral universe bending toward justice. Shifts in ideology eclipsed what was once understood as "natural" and "normal."

In addition to content, how a story is structured is also a seemingly objective, but actually ideological choice. In their 1999 analysis of entertainment media, Silverblatt, Ferry, and Finan draw attention to the ways in which television and movies cater to our society's desire for instant gratification, simplistic notions of good and evil, and a privileging of the self over the collective in the ways programs are designed. Consuming media that train the mind to expect immediate resolution to complex problems promotes an ideology of oversimplification and dichotomous thinking. As Silverblatt, Ferry, and Finan (1999) assert:

> In media programming, the solution to a problem is never far off. To revise an old adage, nothing worth having is worth waiting for. One explanation for the swift resolution to problems can be found in the competitive nature of the media industry. Entertainment programs, in competition for ratings, must attract audiences by holding nothing back. There is no value in patience or subtlety. The preponderance of violence in media programming gives viewers greater doses of instant stimulation to maintain their interest. One clear cumulative message is that violence is indeed an effective solution to problems. Change is swift, immediate, and dramatic [p. 21].

As difficult as ideology masquerading as objective reality in content is to see, it's even more challenging to discern how format both reflects and creates certain ideologies. The aforementioned example illustrates how the ways in which stories are told promote narratives about conflict resolution and violence. There are consequences to consuming media that promote a linear, simplistic view of the world without even making this claim directly. These stories cumulatively become myths, which represent the collective knowledge a society uses to explain phenomena ranging from the human condition to morality. Further, they have a pedagogical function, teaching and socializing in addition to informing. It is therefore critical to understand the ways in which structure privileges certain ideologies while disenfranchising others.

Consumerism emerges as one of the primary ideologies embedded in the seemingly neutral ways media are formatted. Like mainstream television and movie plots promoting dichotomous thinking and simple, swift resolutions, other forms of media endorse certain ideologies in the way they are structured. Zadie Smith (2010) wrote an insightful piece in the *New York Review of Books* offering an analysis of the effects of Facebook's structure on diversity:

> When a human being becomes a set of data on a website like Facebook, he or she is reduced. Everything shrinks. Individual character. Friendships. Language. Sensibility. In a way it's a transcendent experience: we lose our bodies, our messy feelings, our desires, our fears.... With Facebook, Zuckerberg seems to be trying to create something like a Noosphere, an Internet with one mind, a uniform environment in which it genuinely doesn't matter who you are, as long as you make "choices" (which means, finally, purchases). If the aim is to be liked by more and more people, whatever is unusual about a person gets flattened out. One nation under a format.

What makes Smith's (2010) point so compelling is its fresh take on what can be knee-jerk reactions to new media like Facebook or Twitter. Smith (2010) does not fall into the tired commentary about Facebook impeding the youth's ability to communicate or the amount of time one might waste on the site, both of which could be said about many modern distractions. Her point is much more insightful and complex; she unearths the potentially colonizing impulses of Facebook as a medium that wipes out human variation and replaces it with a template. The template presents as an objective reality of sorts, but is actually the result of ideologically driven choices. More specifically, consumerism is the ideology creating how users experience Facebook and, in turn, redefining core human experiences like what it means to be a friend. One might initially think this is an overreaction, but consider the reaction that relationship statuses, for instance, receive on Facebook. We've heard students on many occasions refer to their relationships as "Facebook-official." The point here is not to debate whether Facebook is a good or bad development. Like any other significant innovation ranging from the telephone to the automobile, Facebook both positively and negatively changes the world, oftentimes in ways we cannot even anticipate. What matters here is that people should gain access to the media literacy tools they need to make informed choices about the extent to which they want to engage with media like Facebook. Understanding that their Facebook experience is largely determined by a consumer agenda seems an important first step in making this kind of decision.

Ideology often carries negative connotations because of its association with bias, but once bias is understood as inevitable, we can see that ideology is actually a good, positive, and useful concept. Terms like "balance" and "neutrality" receive undeserved positive implications, but like "moderation," they are actually deeply problematic because they serve to obscure ideology. Ideology masquerading as objective reality serves the interests of the status quo, who only benefit from the ability to obfuscate their agenda. The following section demonstrates how this process works.

Power

The reason media literacy is such a crucial component of any social justice curriculum is that students cannot understand how the status quo is maintained without being exposed to the role of media in reality construction. Otherwise, it makes no sense that slavery, for example, was ever tolerated. Without comprehending how the status quo gains complicity from both agent and target groups through framing issues in accordance with its self-interest, issues like racism make no sense. Indeed, the vast majority of people now disagree with overtly racist statements not because they woke up one day and saw the light, but because the Civil Rights

Movement changed our collective consciousness. Slavery as natural and attempts to escape slavery as abnormal were exposed as beliefs espoused to uphold the status quo, not as objective realities. Most important, once people exposed these policies as decisions rather than natural laws, they could begin the process of changing them.

While hindsight is generally clarifying, seeing the power dimension in the taken-for-granted assumptions in contemporary issue framing proves decidedly more difficult. Part of the reason for this is that the process of attempting neutrality ends up positioning the status quo as a baseline reality of sorts. University of Texas professor of journalism Robert Jensen (2004) provides a powerful illustration of this phenomenon:

> First, it is clear that neutrality is selectively applied. No one would want journalists who are neutral on, say, the routine use of torture on children who misbehave in school, or whether the Holocaust was morally wrong. I assume we would all want journalists who are outraged by these cruelties and would channel that outrage into vigorous reporting. Those examples cause us little concern, for there is wide agreement. But when the issues get stickier—whether or not U.S. forces in Yugoslavia engaged in war crimes, for example—mainstream journalists not only are not allowed to be neutral, but must get in step with the powerful in society; the working assumption was that the United States could not be guilty of war crimes. Claiming to be neutral, then, is simply a cover for adherence to the status quo and the opinions of the powerful [pp. 23–24].

Power, then, is often embedded in the taken-for-granted assumptions that provide the foundation for any kind of story, particularly a news story. These assumptions aren't random; they're designed to evoke thoughts and feelings that adhere to the dominant narrative about a particular issue or topic. This does not mean there is a sinister mastermind behind every news story, slanting it intentionally in one direction or the other. But media are like other institutions in society in terms of their interconnectedness with power centers that determine their viability. In addition, journalists are human beings whose minds were formed by the same hierarchical educational, religious, and corporate entities that provide the power base in our society. Failure to acknowledge how these institutions influence one another requires abdicating responsibility for becoming responsible media consumers.

Conflating neutrality with the interests of the powerful has been an issue in the media for a long time. In the seminal media studies work *Making News*, Gaye Tuchman (1978) articulates the ways in which the status quo's activities are covered as important while "innovative delegitimating social movements are novelties—unless they portend violence and are recast as potential disruptions" (p. 135). Jensen (2004) and Tuchman (1978) demonstrate how the concept of neutrality is fluid, shifting with political winds and powerful interests. This said, it can be easy to slip into a "they're all the same"–type argument and choose not to stay informed on the pertinent issues of our day. This is not the point we're attempting to make. On the contrary, greater participation in media is one of the benefits of today's digital age and quite possibly the hope for more accurate and nuanced reporting. Similarly, the ability to research easily who has controlling interest in a media company and how that might influence the way certain types of stories are framed helps in keeping media honest. The answer is not refusal to engage with media, but rather to do so thoughtfully as an active participant, not a passive consumer.

Tools

One of the most important, yet rarely discussed, concepts in media literacy is the idea of the "bewildered herd." Coined by prominent journalist Walter Lippman in the 1920s, "bewildered herd" (Chomsky, 2002, p. 16) refers to the masses, that part of the population considered too ignorant to think critically or have any voice in important issues. Though politically liberal, Lippman was hostile to the idea of democracy, deeming most people incapable of intelligent participation in civic life. He had much company, with many other journalists, philosophers, and political leaders espousing the same kind of derisive attitude about democracy. The "bewildered herd" concept contains many layers, the primary one being the maintenance of a small elite through keeping the masses distracted with what Noam Chomsky calls, in Wintonick and Achbar's (1992) documentary *Manufacturing Consent*, "emotionally potent oversimplifications, superficial things of life, and necessary illusions." When control cannot be exercised overtly, those in power maintain authority through dumbing down information and promoting mindless consumerism rather than providing thoughtful analysis and thorough coverage of issues in media. Any social justice education curriculum must expose how the media are complicit in upholding the status quo in this manner. Fortunately, there are ways social justice educators can combat these undemocratic and socially unjust practices.

Helping Students Learn Standards of Legitimacy and Credibility

The most obvious, yet often overlooked, way social justice educators can help students become more savvy media consumers is simply to teach them to learn how to decipher legitimate and credible sources. Like objective reality itself, notions of legitimacy and credibility are shifting targets, but there are standards against which these factors can be measured. Paul and Elder (2006) developed useful criteria for evaluating reasoning, which include asking the following questions, adapted for space and clarity:

1. Is the writer's purpose clear and justifiable?
2. Does the writer ask good questions?

3. Does the writer cite accurate and relevant evidence?

4. Does the text reflect the complexity of the issue?

5. Does the text show a sensitivity to what he or she is taking for granted or assuming?

6. Does the writer acknowledge alternative points of view?

7. Does the writer develop a line of reasoning explaining how he or she arrived at his or her main conclusion?

Teaching students to assess a text's legitimacy and credibility using these criteria takes very little time in the course of a semester and produces lasting results. Countless students have told us how they will "never look at media the same way" after completing a relatively short assignment critiquing a text with the aforementioned criteria. These questions are not necessarily life-changing or particularly deep, but they can be instrumental in changing habits. Rather than mindlessly taking in all the media with which we're bombarded on a daily basis, simple exposure to these questions gets students into the habit of consuming media through a critical lens.

In addition to critical questions, some of the literature on groupthink, obedience, and social influence can provide a wealth of material useful for teaching students how to determine legitimacy and credibility. This literature tends to be provocative and stimulating, which can make it a powerful source of knowledge likely to remain with the student past the end of a particular course or program. We've had success using Phillip Zimbardo's (2007) work on the Stanford Prison experiment and the documentary *Quiet Rage* (Musen & Zimbardo, 1992) to illustrate the importance of clear metrics when assessing legitimacy and credibility in both explicitly social justice–oriented classes and courses ranging from group dynamics to organizational theory. Zimbardo essentially ran an "experiment" to investigate conflict between students playing roles as prison guards and inmates and greatly underestimated the impressionability and obedience of people when they are provided with a legitimizing ideology that is reinforced with institutional structures and social supports. Stanley Milgram's (1974) experiments, where participants were asked to obey authority and administer shocks to others, similarly illustrated the tremendous power that environmental factors like legitimizing dogma, authoritative structures, and prestige can have on motivating people to act against their personal conscience. Engaging in reflective discussion with students to challenge the passive acceptance of what happened in the Stanford Prison and Milgram experiments is critical. Further, drilling down into specifically what went wrong in both the Stanford Prison and Milgram experiments assists students in understanding how "normal" people can be manipulated if they are not proactive in deciding for themselves what makes a person or situation credible.

Zimbardo (2007) connects his past work on the Stanford Prison Experiment and more recent work helping the military avoid situations like the Abu Ghraib scandal to Robert Cialdini's work on social influence. Adapted for space and context, the following tenets provide guidance to students' thought process when confronted with authority figures either in person or text:

1. Use critical thinking to separate legitimate and illegitimate authority. Get beyond the superficial trappings like suits, titles, and so on to determine whether to accept someone's expertise.

2. Use critical thinking to ask for support of assertions, to separate rhetoric and conclusion, and develop means-versus-ends thinking.

3. Understand one's own capacity for good and evil. This is particularly useful when processing situations like the Stanford Prison Experiment and Milgram Experiment, where students tend to overestimate their critical thinking skills.

4. Cultivate a perspective about time that connects present decisions to values developed in the past and to an audience

to whom you might have to answer in the future. An example might be imagining having to explain one's lack of support of same-sex marriage at a future time when this might look as closed minded as those who failed to support interracial marriage appear in our contemporary worldview on the topic.

5. Develop your position on an issue with an understanding of the context and framing.

As with the critical questions, these tenets have the potential to create good habits in students' consumption of media, transforming them from passive recipients to active agents. Armed with the tools they need to examine critically and thoughtfully the media to which they are exposed, students can become more proactive in deciding what they deem credible and legitimate information sources.

Saving the Humanities Has to Be a Social Justice Issue We Take On

Higher education exists, in part, to create informed citizens capable of participating in democracy. While steeped in the racism, classism, and sexism of its earliest days, higher education institutions nonetheless embraced clearly defined missions of advancing the public good through the intellectual and moral development of their students. These missions were often religious in nature and often problematically so, but they provided a space in which students could wrestle with philosophical and ethical issues.

During the Industrial Revolution, the corporation replaced the church as the dominant institution in the United States, changing forever virtually every aspect of society, including universities. The changing socioeconomic conditions of the mid-nineteenth century stimulated a dramatic shift in this original purpose of higher education in the United States, motivating the newly created capitalists to become interested in universities as a means to train specialized workers in this new economy. The land-grant movements of the 1860s marked the first official law in a series of legislation tying the interests and purposes of the university to those of big business. Although the land-grant movement did in fact extend the opportunity for higher education to a wider population, it also marked the erosion of the idea of an education as valuable in its own right. Washburn (2005) provides an insightful analysis of how the interests of the economic sector appropriated the original purposes of higher education: "Unfortunately, though it [the land grant movement] unquestionably brought benefits and helped to modernize the university, this new emphasis on utility also fostered an unmistakable strain of anti-intellectualism ... All too many universities embraced a crude vocationalism, allowing academic standards to erode, equating education with mere training, and forgetting that the quest for knowledge had intrinsic worth" (p. 31). These conflicts of interest between educating citizens and training workers are only more present today. Volumes have been written about higher education losing its center in an increasingly bottom-line-driven environment (Arum, 2011; Bok, 2003; Hacker & Dreifus, 2010; Hersh & Merrow, 2006; Kirp, 2003; Lagemann, 2012; Taylor, 2010; Tuchman, 2009; Zemsky, Wegner & Massy, 2006). This point is not meant as an indictment of the economic benefits of a college degree; we support those. But we question why preparing students for careers in private industry and citizenship in public society are so often framed as mutually exclusive.

This is a question Nussbaum (2010) addresses in *Not for Profit*, an excellent treatise on the vital role of the humanities in promoting and sustaining democracy: "But educators for economic growth will do more than ignore the arts. They will fear them. For a cultivated and developed sympathy is a particularly dangerous enemy of obtuseness, and moral obtuseness is necessary to carry out programs of economic development that ignore inequality. It is easier to treat people as objects to be manipulated if you have not learned any other way to see them" (p. 23). The slow erosion of the humanities has enormous implications for both media literacy specifically and social justice generally. Once we accept higher education as a private commodity as opposed to a public good (as illustrated through declining public funding of higher education), we lose one of the few spaces in our society where people can learn the skills they need to unpack the often hegemonic media to which they are exposed on a daily basis. These skills include understanding how language works, a crucial component in media literacy. Students need spaces to learn, for example, how calling something an "estate tax" versus a "death tax" alters the meaning people will ascribe to a particular policy. They need to grapple with the ways language is used to desensitize (for example, a term like "collateral damage") and frame issues (for example, whether to refer to areas in the Middle East as "Palestine" or "the occupied territories" or a host of other terms that offer a range of different connotations.) Other disciplines certainly offer valuable skills, but the humanities are uniquely positioned to teach students to think critically, work through ambiguity, and express nuance in ways unlikely to occur in more linear, concrete, applied fields. These are the very capacities needed to offset an increasingly polarized, sound bite–oriented, and reductive media.

Nussbaum (2010) offers a compelling argument for making the connection between the fate of the humanities and social justice in higher education. Social justice educators tend to do an excellent job of advocating for students of color, women, economically disenfranchised, and LGBT students' inclusion in higher education, but what does it matter if the substance of that education is so compromised that students leave institutions without the enhanced critical thinking skills to participate fully in an advanced democracy? Ensuring equal access to the educational institutions fueling the economic engines in our society is a legitimate social justice issue, but it doesn't get to the deeper issues of what an education ought to be. If a social justice agenda stops short of advocating for an education that would teach students how to question the inequalities inherent in the economic engine itself, we could do more harm by encouraging participation in a system that actively works against the interests of particular groups of people.

Finally, the erosion of the humanities is problematic because it creates a meaning vacuum in students' educational experience. This happens at the subtext level in much the same way that the structuring of television and movie narratives promotes linear, quick-fix thinking. Similarly, academic experiences devoid of the humanities aren't necessarily designed to diminish students' search for meaning, but this is a by-product nonetheless. In his important work on this topic, Kronman (2007) addresses the point of the humanities: "The answer is that we need the humanities to meet the deepest spiritual longing of our age, whose roots lie in the hegemony of science itself" (p. 229). We have collectively witnessed countless socially unjust results of the hegemony of science devoid of a corresponding attention to meaning. Eugenics, wars conducted with desensitized distance, and a surveillance society are just a few examples of the kinds of consequences that result from an uneven focus on technological advancement without the accompanying moral reasoning to ensure the socially responsible use of these developments. Understanding, valuing, and advocating for the humanities are important steps in fostering educational environments supportive of the critical thinking skills necessary to promote social justice in our contemporary world, where the issues are increasingly complex.

Representation

This chapter opened with a story about examining the ways in which media represent a group of people. This is too often where analyses of media and social justice begin and end, yet representation remains a significant issue in media literacy. The issue is far more important than simply what offends or passes some sort of benign political correctness test. Said (2001), correctly in our view, identifies violence and consumption as the critical issues at stake when he writes: "The act of representing (and hence reducing) others almost always involves violence of some sort to the subject of the representation, as well as a contrast between the act of the violence representing something and the calm exterior of the representation itself, the image—verbal, visual, or otherwise—of the subject … because, above all, representation involves consumption" (p. 40). Said's (2001) words reflect the seriousness of the ways in which media, largely controlled by powerful interests, represent people. Representation evokes emotion on the part of the consumer, heightening or diminishing empathy based on how circumstances are framed. These feelings in turn lead to thoughts and opinions that drive behaviors that have real consequences, such as how people vote or whether to make a charitable donation to a particular cause. Examples abound, such as the popular image of the "welfare queen" in the 1980s. Media representations of impoverished single mothers as manipulating systems drove popular opinion about their worthiness, which in turn led to policies eviscerating the welfare system under Presidents Reagan, Bush, and Clinton. "Ending welfare as we know it" became a popular mantra, despite the fact that Aid to Families with Dependent Children requires far less of the federal budget than the massive amounts of money spent on corporate welfare, for example (Barlett & Steele, 1998; Sinn, 2012). More recent examples can be seen in situations such as the disparity between how the victims of 9/11 and Hurricane Katrina were represented in the mainstream media and how public opinion and support differed in response. As these examples demonstrate, representation does not simply reflect a certain reality; it creates and delimits possibilities.

While there is much of which to be skeptical in media, the violence Said (2001) articulated as part of representation can be destructive, such as in war, or it can be creative, such as in birth. While media representations can limit people's possibilities, they can also expand worlds, giving voice to experiences people may believe they are feeling in isolation. Linne (2007) provides an example of the ways in which queer media facilitate the coming out process for many LGBT people: "For young queers, learning the discourse very often begins with the media. Many coming out stories include memories of a favorite character from a book on which the young reader closely studied and patterned parts of her or his emerging persona. Like a drag performer putting on a Hollywood version of hyper-femininity, young queers might try on roles they see portrayed in media culture—some empowering, some self-destructive" (p. 465). These words capture the heart of issues of representation specifically and media more generally; namely, that these are tools that can be used for creation or destruction based on the capabilities and inclinations of the hands that hold them. People create what they consume, which can lead to a cycle of social injustice without critical analysis of the media that colors all of our perceptions.

Conclusion

Understanding media plays a vital role in twenty-first-century social justice education. Considering the ways in which media construct our emotions, attitudes, and behaviors, one can begin to identify some sources of resistance to aspects of the complex social justice issues that define the post–Civil Rights, post–Women's Movement era. While things were far from simple in the Civil Rights and second-wave feminist movement years, blatant inequality and legal discrimination were easier to identify as justice issues. Issues like the ongoing need for affirmative action despite having elected the first black president or how uneven school funding leads to unequal opportunities are more nuanced social justice issues requiring more nuanced information than that typically offered by the linear, reductive mainstream media. Helping students access alternative sources of knowledge in addition to consuming mainstream media with a critical mind are vital components of contemporary social justice education.

7

Disrupting Organizational Practices to Empower People

> I'm sad to report that in the past few years, ever since
> uncertainty became our insistent 21st century companion,
> leadership has taken a great leap backwards to the familiar
> territory of command and control.
> —Margaret J. Wheatley (2006)

Because it is so difficult to successfully implement a critical pedagogy, contesting rigid institutions to embrace social justice practices can feel overwhelming. Achieving substantive, sustainable change in organizations is one of the biggest challenges in social justice work. One-time programs or initiatives have their place, but larger systemic change proves difficult to enact. Cosmetic alterations to an existing structure tend to be tolerated; a popular example might be the common practice of using photographs of diverse students in college admissions materials. There is value in making sure multicultural students are visually represented in a college's literature, but this does not necessarily help the vision of greater higher education access come to fruition. Educational equity, like any other social justice issue, requires knowledge of organizational theory so that systems can first be seen and understood, then negotiated and ultimately changed.

Understanding organizational theory is important to social justice work for two key reasons. The first is that efforts that don't address change at the systemic level often yield shallow results, which lead to justifiable criticisms, such as those frequently made by students of color when they see admissions brochures that look like they are for historically black colleges and universities (HBCUs), but upon arrival at a campus they find they are severely underrepresented. The second reason organizational theory is integral to social justice work is that diversity issues are far more complex than people tend to articulate. While people may have the best intentions in working for social change, they can end up actually hurting the cause without careful attention to the larger systemic issues at play in a given situation.

An excellent example of this phenomenon occurs when people from the United States want to effect change on behalf of disenfranchised people in developing countries. People's hearts are generally in the right place, but often their failure to comprehend the complicated structures and systems in both the potential recipients of their aid and their own organizations thwarts such efforts. As a result, predominantly white, Western aid organizations can get reputations for being cumbersome, unhelpful, and sometimes patronizing, though their stated aims are the opposite. Unchecked assumptions about how one's organization ought to approach its work can be as antithetical to one's goals as mistakes in carrying out the work itself.

Fortunately, being proactive in defining and reevaluating the systemic realities in one's organization can mitigate the aforementioned problems. Anne Firth Murray, founder of the Global Fund for Women, provides a living example of a person who built an organization on very different assumptions from those that define most institutions. I (Harrison) describe her work here because it provides such a powerful illustration of the good things that can happen when people break out of conventional paradigms of what it means to lead an organization. I got to know Anne during my years at Stanford University, where she taught courses on international women's health and love as a force for social change. Anne's classes were extremely popular; it took students most of their undergraduate career to get into her classes. Given the bounty of interesting classes Stanford offers, I was intrigued by this phenomenon and asked several students why they worked so hard to get into Anne's classes. The responses tended to fall into two themes: relevance and respect. Students were in awe of both the Global Fund for Women's accomplishments and the way Anne ignored routine classroom hierarchies and offered students agency in their own learning. The more I got to know Anne and what went on in both her organization and her classroom, the more I began to see how these phenomena were thoroughly connected to each other and to an alternative approach to theorizing organizations in both educational and philanthropic contexts.

The first, most noticeable way in which the Global Fund for Women manifests an alternative vision of organizational theory is that it is centered on issues identified by women in developing countries, not Anne or her colleagues' notions about what these women need. The Global Fund for Women provides grants that support women's empowerment as defined by the women themselves. The attitude reflected in this approach cultivates respect and builds credibility among the women who experience agency in a system that seeks their input, rather than trying to impose an outside agenda.

Another way in which Anne's organization exemplifies a nontraditional approach to management is through her enfranchisement of young people in leadership positions. Interestingly, this practice initially raised suspicion among some board members whose assumptions led them to believe there must be some reason other than Anne's belief in these young peoples' talents motivating this practice. As she explained,

> A couple of my board members questioned my hiring so many young people and particularly my giving them real responsibilities; the board members accused me of

> doing this in order to maintain power. This suggestion surprised and saddened me, not only because they missed the point of my actions but because they demeaned the wonderful contributions of these young staff members. Simply put, my reasons for hiring such young people were that they had fresh perspectives, they were not likely to second-guess the women who were writing from around the world, and they brought different experiences and expertise that greatly benefited the organization. Perhaps most important, the young staff people were especially eager to learn from the women who wrote to us [Murray, 2006, p. 95].

Centering an organization around the needs of the people it was designed to serve and empowering its workers may seem like obvious components to success. So why are they so rarely implemented, even in organizations with social justice missions? Why do so many organizations fail to act in the interests of the people they purportedly exist to serve? Why do so many workers and managers express disenchantment with one another, constantly questioning one another's motivations and agendas? The following section attempts to answer these questions by outlining the ways in which conventional mental models about organizations create unnecessary and artificial divisions between people. The chapter concludes with an analysis of some of the cutting-edge organizational theories that can help organizations move toward practices that produce truly innovative work such as that carried out by the Global Fund for Women.

Conventional Organizational Practices

A significant challenge in studying organizations is that they present themselves as benignly rational. Unless an organization makes the news, such as when the CEO of Chick-fil-A made negative comments about same-sex marriage, our tendency is not to think about the organizations with which we interact on a daily basis. Even in Chick-fil-A's case, the national conversation is about an individual's position on an issue, not the daily operations of the organization. We accept general organizational features like chains of command and focus on efficiency as natural, yet these practices and many other modern-day management techniques came from theories very much connected to slavery and colonialism (Brewis & Jack, 2011). This reality, coupled with the ways in which the ubiquity of mainstream managerial practices generally conceal this fact, serve to mask the power relations that define the vast majority of organizations' systems and structures.

Morgan (2006) unpacks the idea of organizations as rational enterprises and shows how this line of thinking conceals the truly political nature of them. He shows how what should be obvious questions are obfuscated by the notion that organizations are driven by simple, uncomplicated goals like efficiency and productivity. Moreover, Morgan (2006) reveals the ideological nature of organizations, pointing out the shifting nature of what becomes constructed as rational based on whose interests are being served. Morgan writes, "Organizations may pursue goals and stress the importance of rational, efficient, and effective management. But rational, efficient, and effective for whom? Whose goals are being pursued? What interests are being served? Who benefits? The political metaphor emphasizes that organizational goals may be rational for some people's interests but not for others. An organization embraces many rationalities because rationality is always interest based and thus changes according to the perspective from which it is viewed. Rationality is always political" (p. 203). He exposes the fallacy that organizations operate according to principles of fixed rationality. He also shows how what appears to be an objective reality in organizational life is actually an ideology bendable to the will of those who preserve the status quo. In order for this status quo to be maintained, it is important for those in power to conceal the reality of organizations as political entities so that they can create the illusion that institutional systems operate according to objective principles that will somehow benefit all, or at the very least, the most worthy.

Technical Rationality

How organizations are theorized is not simply an academic matter, because how a system is designed affects what it will produce, which has enormous implications for social justice. Adams and Balfour's (2009) work entitled *Unmasking Administrative Evil* lays out a compelling argument for explaining how the modern organization contributed to atrocities like the Holocaust through its fundamentalist focus on efficiency. While violence and oppression certainly took place before the Holocaust, they argue that the widespread compliance of people who did not necessarily buy into its vision was made possible by the idea of technical rationality. They define technical rationality as "a way of thinking and living that elevates the scientific-analytical mindset and the belief in technological progress over all other forms of rationality. Indeed, it becomes synonymous with rationality itself" (p. 30). Adams and Balfour (2009) go on to show how the dominance of technical rationality creates a social reality that contrasts with substantive rationality, which they define as "the ability to understand the purposeful nature of the whole system of which a particular task is a part" (p. 30). They hypothesize that the predominance of technical rationality provides the foundation for what they call administrative evil—the moral wrong of which people are unwittingly capable in their everyday roles and functions within an organization. If what counts is how efficiently one does his or her job (technical rationality), rather than whether or not one is doing the right things on the job (substantive rationality), then it becomes clear how otherwise sane individuals become capable of committing atrocities in organizational contexts. While organizations are generally not exclusively technically or substantively rational, a lack of attention to the difference can lead to a dangerous slipping toward mechanical efficiency that ignores fundamental purpose and direction.

By painting a picture of organizations as benignly rational and therefore politically neutral, those in power can convince large numbers of people to go along with an agenda they do not even know, much less share. Couching ideology in the language of "business as usual" creates a situation in which people will comply without even making an active choice. As Adams and Balfour (2009) point out, the average worker in Germany did not even belong to the Nazi party, yet conceptualizing work through the lens of technical rationality created a situation in which people focused on efficiency and productivity rather than the nature of the work itself. The hidden power dynamic in this organizational reality epitomizes the idea of cultural hegemony by naturalizing an agenda as simply "following orders" or "doing one's job." Furthermore, Adams and Balfour (2009) explain that the Holocaust itself was made possible not just by the people who actually hated Jews and actively sought their demise, but by regular people in the course of their everyday business:

> The nature and dynamics of these deadly bureau-
> cratic processes are not unique to Nazi Germany or
> the Holocaust, but are entirely consistent with mod-
> ern organizations and the technical-rational approach
> to administration. The significance of the connection
> between the Holocaust and the civil service in Germany
> is such that responsibility for the event extends not only
> to the central perpetrators who planned and committed
> overt acts of killing innocent human beings, but also to
> thousands of ordinary public administrators carrying out
> seemingly routine and neutral tasks [pp. 43–44].

There are many more modern examples of this idea of individuals somehow losing their moral compass in the service of a

sinister goal cloaked in the idea of the organization as rational enterprise. Judith Stone (2007), for instance, unpacked the system of apartheid through the lens of one of its victims, Sandra Laing, in a work about how those not clearly identifiable as white or black were treated in apartheid South Africa. While the book is primarily about the arbitrariness of race, Stone does an excellent job of illustrating how ordinary people perpetuated a system now understood as deeply wrong. In her account, Stone (2007) records a story of one of the bureaucrats responsible for race classification:

> I say I was the registrar of births, deaths, and marriages. Who is anybody to judge another? We broke up families. All the time I was working in the department I was very glad I was white.... I did feel pity at the time but it was a job. I had to earn my living.... We didn't make the final decision, we just made the recommendations. Humanity didn't come into our recommendations. We had to stick to the rules—the tragedy didn't influence us. We would have situations where children with the same parents ended up with different classifications.... I am an Afrikaner through and through. But race classification was wrong. I am not proud of what I did. But I can't say I am ashamed. There was nothing we could do about it. I'm just glad it's over [p. 206].

These are just two examples of how technical rationality can lead to organizational horrors when values-free efficiency is the only metric. Technical rationality relies on strict adherence to chains of commands, or hierarchies, to implement its vision of absolute efficiency at any cost. The need for chains of command is taken for granted and yet the aforementioned illustrations demonstrate that they often do more harm than good.

Hierarchy

Understanding the relationship between technical rationality and hierarchy is crucial in our contemporary culture, where efficiency at any cost is the ethos of the day. Rarely are people allowed to stop and ask whether their organization is doing the right things; instead they ask whether they are doing them faster and more productively than their competitors. Seemingly neutral words like *efficiency* conflate the elite's interests with those of the greater good. Nord and Jermier (1999) articulate how language can be used to hide agendas by framing them as objective: "Many managers are especially intrigued by discovering the obfuscation inherent in certain terms from everyday business discourse such as efficiency. Generally, people will agree that efficiency is defined as output divided by input. When one raises the question about what outputs are to be included (pollution, job-related illnesses, and so on), it is clear that the normal indices represent a particular set of interests and that the word *efficiency* is loaded with political content" (p. 206).

The ability to expose the ways in which the status quo maintains its power—through making it appear as though its interests are the same as what the Occupy Movement called "the 99 percent"—is at the heart of social justice education. Too often, we focus on the targets of oppression rather than the agents, which leads to confusion about why racism, classism, sexism, and so on persist, when almost no one will advocate these prejudices openly. Uneven emphasis on targeted groups allows the agents to carry on unquestioned and unchallenged. We need to drill down deep to understand how the agents' systems function, as well as the assumptions underlying their operating principles.

One key assumption critical to revealing how hierarchical social arrangements are allowed to continue is the notion of inevitability. Power relations manifest in hierarchies, which appear as natural orders that have always existed. The ahistorical approach most management and leadership studies curricula take to examining hierarchy reinforces this notion of them as inevitable. In fact, people have organized themselves into various kinds of social configurations, the chain-of-command model not formally existing until Frederick the Great of Prussia popularized it in the mid-1700s. It's worth noting that the chain-of-command model was born of a very specific history involving a leader who inherited a band of criminals as his army and needed to find ways to control them (Vercic & Grunig, 2000). This history alone warrants a reconsideration of the often mindless acceptance of hierarchy as the default that continues to define the vast majority of contemporary organizations.

Inevitability as a default assumption allows hierarchy to function unquestioned as baseline normalcy. As a result, people can be convinced to accept a paradigm that actively works against their own interests because they do not perceive a choice. Hierarchies serve to naturalize power relations in order to keep them hidden and therefore not subject to scrutiny or debate. As Knights (2011) explains, "power is not just about removing potentials for conflict off the agenda but also involves defining the situation such that subordinates internalize norms and comply even when it is against their interests to do so" (p. 147). Thus, people often end up unwittingly supporting or even defending their own oppressors because they accept the status quo's interests as objective reality. Given the ways in which the elite appropriate language, history, and institutional norms and practices, it should not be difficult at this point to see how this happens.

As a result, people rarely question or challenge the existing social order because they cannot see the power dynamics at work in it. On the rare occasion that they do raise questions, those in power immediately dismiss these ideas as impractical or impossible. When people discuss hierarchy, for example, they may not like it, but they tend to preempt creative ideas about alternatives by self-policing themselves into the conviction that there isn't any other way to maintain order. Those in power capitalize on these fears, convincing us to accept hierarchy as the price for order without considering that order, like efficiency, may be a concept that appears as benignly neutral but that is actually politically loaded. Writing at the height of the Civil Rights and Vietnam War protests, Zinn (1968) shed light on the shifting nature of what order means depending on one's status: "Thus, exactly at that moment when we have begun to suspect that law is congealed injustice, that the existing order hides an everyday violence against body and spirit, that our political structure is fossilized, and that the noise of change—however scary—may be necessary, a cry rises for 'law and order'" (p. 4). Zinn rightly pointed out that both order and violence carry disparate meanings depending on the targets and agents of these concepts. While the existing order at the time worked for some members of society, it actively oppressed others whose only option was to challenge it. Hierarchical systems resist conflict for obvious reasons, yet the only path to change requires identifying and disrupting systems that serve only to benefit the status quo at the expense of the common good. This is true even when those caught in the mental model of an existing order do not seek to be oppressive, as in the case of Western aid organizations described earlier. The only way to get to fresh solutions and creative thinking is to theorize organizations that support goals other than the blind submission required in chain-of-command hierarchies. Fortunately, alternative approaches to conventional organizational theory do exist and prove useful in the service of a social justice vision.

Systems Approach to Organizations

One of the many problems with the ways in which organizations have been conventionally theorized is their tendency toward reduction. Indeed, classical organizational theory is defined by reducing wholes to parts, as one might understand a machine (Shafritz, Ott, & Jang, 2005). Likening organizations to machines makes sense, given classical organizational theory's roots in the zeitgeist of the Industrial Revolution. Reducing a whole to its parts may be effective in fixing a machine or developing an assembly line; however, this approach creates a host of problems when applied to more complex organizational contexts. First, as the previously discussed examples of unchecked technical rationality demonstrate, blind focus on one part of a system allows people to abdicate responsibility for the organization's greater impact. If I am responsible only for processing this set of forms or delivering that paperwork, it doesn't matter to what end my work is a means.

The second problem with trying to understand something as complex as a contemporary organization as merely the sum total of its parts is that this leads to misdiagnoses of organizational problems. Too often, people attribute blame hastily because they fail to see the layered, patterned nature of how systems work. Wheatley (2006) offers the following explanation: "A system is composed of parts, but we cannot understand a system by looking only at its parts. We need to work with the whole of a system, even as we work with individual parts or isolated problems. From a systems consciousness, we understand that no problem or behavior can be understood in isolation. We must account for dynamics operating in the whole system that are displaying themselves in these individual moments" (pp. 139–140). An excellent example of this can be seen in family systems counseling, which developed in response to more individually focused approaches' failure to address core problems within families. A typical example might be two parents bringing an unruly teenager to counseling in hopes that the therapist will fix the problem as they define it, meaning within the adolescent. Family systems counselors will treat the teenager, but will also examine the broader context of the family dynamic to see how the child's behavior connects to what is happening with the parents as well. The counselor may find that the parents have marital problems that get pushed aside when the adolescent acts out, creating a cycle that actually reinforces the teen's behavior because it brings the parents together. The point here is that isolating a problem and examining it out of context rarely yields the kind of sophisticated diagnosis needed to truly understand complicated systemic issues.

The final problem with reductive approaches to organizations is that they preempt potentially creative solutions with linear thinking incapable of challenging existing paradigms. Shallow diagnoses lead to overly simplified responses to complicated organizational conundrums. As a result, Band-aid solutions that fail to provide more sustainable change and/or heavy-handed control measures that alienate people can become defaults that impede substantive progress. Fortunately, organizational theory is ahead of organizational practice and can provide some guideposts for understanding and operating in organizations more holistically.

Holistic Approaches

In contrast to the partial and distorted diagnoses that occur in reductive approaches, holistic approaches to organizations allow members to make more informed choices about the consequences of their actions. Ecological examples provide the clearest illustration of this reality, and the case of DDT in mosquito eradication is frequently cited to demonstrate the point (Ollhoff & Walcheski, 2002). A solution born of linear thinking about a problem viewed out of context, the use of DDT not only failed to solve the problem, but exacerbated it by killing off mosquitoes' natural predators and building a mosquito population immune to DDT. Extreme focus on efficiency and chain of command would have people pumping as much DDT into the environment as quickly and thoroughly as possible without questioning how this solution affects the bigger picture—which in turn affects the project at hand. In a closed system where the whole is reduced to shortsighted initiatives that fail to account for all the other variables involved, efficiency prevails at the expense of effectiveness.

There are countless other examples of well-intended interventions that prove the old "cure as worse than the disease" adage.

In fact, when people ponder deep systemic problems like failing schools or skyrocketing national deficits, the problem can almost always be traced back to what Kegan and Lahey (2009) call immunity to change. Much like the previous example of the teenager in family therapy, what appears to be dysfunctional behavior on the surface can be highly functional in a system where the behavior yields desired results like marital harmony. Conventional models of organizations theorize people as existing in competition with one another, but systems approaches understand individuals' fates as deeply connected. Therefore, the only way to understand the teenager in the family is to understand how her or his behavior affects and is affected by the other members of the household. Otherwise, much like the DDT-mosquito scenario, we are likely to design interventions that either fail to address the deeper systemic issues or actually worsen the situation.

Part of the reason a holistic approach is so vital to theorizing organizations more effectively is that it requires individuals to see their role in both problems and solutions. Unlike the cases described in the technical rationality section, individuals cannot abdicate responsibility in a holistic view of organizations because they are not merely parts of a whole; they *are* the whole. Senge (1994) articulates an important distinction between understanding problems in blame-versus-contribution paradigms. Blame paradigms are possible in models where wholes are mere sums of parts, because parts exist in competition with one another. When a problem or issue occurs, the tendency is to isolate it from other parts of the organization, identify what Senge (1994) calls "the patient," and treat or punish it depending on the situation at hand. In a holistic paradigm, individuals take responsibility for the organization and are therefore assumed to have contributed to both problems and solutions. As a result, people are more likely to engage in honest, meaningful conversations about real issues at work, rather than saving those for the water cooler or happy hour, making real change people can buy into more of a possibility (Scharmer, 2007).

Interconnectedness

Only when people deal with a problem holistically—including their role in it—is true change possible. Conventional organizational theory emphasizes separateness of people and problems, individuals and organizations, classes of people within organizations, and inside of organizations and the outside world. Holistic approaches to organizations posit connectedness not only as important, but as the basis of reality (Katz & Kahn, 2005). This is perhaps the most important distinction between conventional and systems approaches to organizational theory in terms of social justice. When all that is real is me, my agenda, and my small part of an organization, I am very likely to view anything outside of these things as threats. When I understand my fate as integrally connected to what happens to the people with whom I share a home, neighborhood, community, and ultimately, a planet, I am incentivized to consider the consequences of my actions on them not only out of benevolence, but out of self-interest as well. The wall between being generous toward others and self-protection is exposed as illusion because what happens to them happens to me and vice versa.

Interconnectedness creates stronger organizations by breaking down the "it's not my job" kind of thinking and allowing a freer exchange of ideas that allows different constituencies to understand the daily realities of other stakeholders within an organization. This kind of approach tends to engender what Buber (1996) called I-Thou relationships; that is, connections based on mutual respect and trust. He contrasted this notion with I-It relationships, which offer agency to only one party while allowing the other to be objectified. Conventional organizational practices objectify both nonelite members of their own organizations and those not relevant to the relentless pursuit of efficiency and control. Consequently, it can be easy for individuals at different levels in an organizational hierarchy to work in a siloed fashion, indifferent to one another's experiences. Senge, Scharmer, Jaworski, and Flowers

(2008) explain how divisions between people limit commitment to a shared vision: "Only when people begin to see from within the forces that shape their reality and to see their part in how these forces might evolve does vision become powerful. Everything else is just vague hope. This is why most visions that management teams come up with are superficial. Even if they embody a lot of good thinking, they're still a product of a fragmented awareness, and usually one or two people's ideas imposed on the group" (p. 132). Without the real buy-in that results when people perceive the benefits of an I-Thou relationship, visions become fodder for parodies like the television series *The Office.* Imposed from "on high," visions that reflect only the voices of the elite class are easy to ignore.

When people are invited to participate in all aspects of an organization, however, they tend to feel more invested as true stakeholders. To return to Anne Firth Murray and the Global Fund for Women, Murray built an organization that connected people rather than separated them. As she explained, "We raised money to give it away, and we did this in such a way that we hoped to blur the lines between givers and receivers" (Murray, 2006, p. xxiv). This practice helped all parts of the organization feel invested in the other parts, as well as stay focused on the vision as the driving force. It also helped the organization avoid some of the pitfalls of other aid organizations by constantly keeping people from getting out of touch or losing sight of the purpose of the work.

Imagine a world in which organizations united rather than divided donors and recipients, management and labor, teachers and students. What social justice progress might be possible if we theorized organizations in such a way that practices like Murray's were more widespread? Would we collectively gain traction on seemingly intractable problems?

Empowerment

One seemingly intractable problem that offers a window into how different organizational theories yield different diagnoses and approaches is student underperformance in public schools. An exhaustive discussion of the various interventions that have been tried is beyond the scope of this chapter, but it's worth highlighting one educational leader whose systems approach to organizational change has produced a school where traditionally underserved students are performing at the highest levels. Deborah Meier, widely considered the founder of the small schools movement, has successfully led several schools in economically disenfranchised parts of New York City and Boston. Unlike many commentators and school reformers who blame teachers, students, and students' parents for underperformance, despite gross inequities in access to resources, Meier looks for what contributes to the problem rather than seeking to blame. Consequently, she spends more time critiquing biases in standardized tests and advocating for a more equitable distribution of resources than blaming overworked and underpaid parents when problems arise. As a result, parental involvement is higher at Meier's schools, where people who are already underserved by society do not risk additional shame by interacting with educational professionals because they treat parents as partners rather than problems.

Like Anne Firth Murray with the Global Fund for Women, Meier exemplifies a nonhierarchical approach in her organizational practice. By refusing to focus solely on efficiency for efficiency's sake or reduce complex problems like racism and poverty to motivation issues, Meier demonstrates absolute respect for the people her organization aims to serve. As Meier (2002) states:

> At the heart of the idea of progressive education is a still unaccepted notion: that giving both adolescents and their teachers greater responsibility for the development of their schools can't be bypassed. Without a radical departure from a more authoritarian model, one strips the key parties of the respect which lies at the heart of democratic practice and good schooling. As long as we see "these kids" as dangers to our civil peace and

> their teachers as time-servers or crazy martyrs, we are
> not likely to offer either group the respect they need to
> make schools work. Schools for thoughtfulness can't be
> built on top of thoughtlessness [p. 35].

By not seeing themselves as separate from the people they seek to both affect and allow themselves to be affected by, Meier and Murray have built progressive organizations that have real impacts in the struggle for gender, racial, and economic justice. Their refusal to reduce both complex issues and individuals' complicated lives to problems to be controlled affords them credibility with the constituents they aim to serve. Their nimble organizations do not suffer from bloated bureaucratic layers that separate people and create missions that only those at the top of a steep hierarchy value or claim as their own. Interestingly, Meier (2002) also wrote of others' mistrust of her commitment to empower people other than those at the highest levels of leadership in her schools. Most people would pay lip service to the goals of either leader's organization, but as their respective books describe, deep, systemic change challenges the status quo and is therefore difficult to implement. The advances in social justice that can occur when change visions at that level are realized, however, make a compelling case for the commitment required to enact truly progressive organizations.

Conclusion

Most people reading this chapter do not plan to found organizations or turn around underperforming schools. But many readers either do or will lead a department or teach a class, and the default most likely to occur to them will be based on conventional management practices of efficiency, order, hierarchy, and reductivism. This isn't because people consciously or proactively buy into these practices; rather, these approaches are presented as the only way to do things. As Murray (2006) and Meier (2002) demonstrate, however, the possibilities for truly creative approaches to old problems come from building organizations that are truly different. These leaders inspire change because their organizations are genuinely future-focused, not relying on past practices as templates for how to achieve their respective visions.

Some people will finish this chapter concluding that "it's a nice idea, but hierarchy is here to stay," and there is some truth in this critique. Although we have written about conventional and systemic approaches to organizations in contrast, lived reality would suggest that they are not either-or propositions. The Global Fund for Women has a board, and Meier's schools have principals; even these progressive organizations do not operate completely flatly without some sort of structure. Similarly, Debra Meyerson's *Tempered Radicals* (2001) and Joe Badaracco's *Leading Quietly* (2002) offer strategies workers can employ to achieve modest, incremental change in conventional organizations. The important point is to see the organizational practices that have been taken for granted for so long or seen as inevitable and make informed choices about how to renegotiate them toward the vision of a more socially just future.

8

Strategies for Reinvigorating Social Justice in Higher Education

The academy is not paradise. But learning is a place where paradise can be created. The classroom with all its limitations remains a location of possibility. In that field of possibility we have the opportunity to labour for freedom, to demand of ourselves and our comrades, an openness of mind and heart that allows us to face reality even as we collectively imagine ways to move beyond boundaries, to transgress. This is education as the practice of freedom.

—*bell hooks (1994, p. 207)*

If we could change ourselves, the tendencies in the world would also change. As a man changes his own nature, so does the attitude of the world change towards him.... We need not wait to see what others do.

—*Mahatma Gandhi*

Gandhi's quote is often reduced to the bumper sticker catchphrase, "Be the change you wish to see in the world." One of the dangers of distilling his original words is that the quote can be interpreted to mean that all one needs to do is focus on oneself. As the powerful feminist slogan reminds us, however, the personal is political. Our interpretation of Gandhi's words—perhaps more powerfully communicated in the catchphrase—is captured in the verb *to be*. What does it mean, for example, to embody or breathe life into change? How can we represent our deepest being, that which connects us all, to transform not just our consciousness, but the world around us? What if we dissolve the false dichotomy constructed in part by positivist tendencies described in the beginning of this book between self and other, between personal and political, to make them one and the same? What, that is, would it look like to *be* the change?

In this chapter, we hope to provide a path toward reinvigorating our work to dissolve the distinction between theory and practice to form a praxis that helps us enact change. Implementing a social justice agenda in higher education is parallel to the challenges of doing so in the larger society. Colleges and universities, in our experience, are ambivalent about change and are much more comfortable designing neoliberal policies and vaguely titled programs that promote "global citizens" and support "diversity" or "community service." But colleges and universities are inhabited and run by people. We believe that individuals willing to employ counterhegemonic practices, as well as balance cognitive critique with empathy, compassion, and critical humility, can succeed in bringing us closer to the kind of equity, liberty, and justice promised in our most fundamental democratic social contract. The social justice concepts outlined throughout this book can serve as road signs, but the journey needs to be navigated by each individual. The concepts cannot be memorized or simply accepted, but must be critically consumed and animated through the actions of each person.

Social action toward justice can be aroused through ideas, but is only realized through real-world performance. Both Harrison and I (Davis) were raised within the Catholic faith, and we have been deeply influenced by the actions of nuns who courageously model the kind of philosophy-to-action praxis necessary for change. We are also profoundly inspired by Eastern ways of being, particularly Zen Buddhism. Buddhism strongly supports the notion that "social imperfections can be reduced by the reduction of greed, hatred, and ignorance, and by compassionate action guided by wisdom" (Jones, 1988, p. 68). Moreover, Buddhist teachings argue for a middle way, a sort of balancing of extremes through mindful effort to reconcile apparent paradoxes. We believe that effective social justice practice in higher education is very much like this dialectic. For example, it is necessary to balance internal reflection with external action, logic with intuition, rationality with passion, individual rights with community liberties, awareness of institutional forces with attention to personal choices, and the social with the psychological. Also consistent with Buddhism is our belief that there are many paths toward consciousness, but all depend upon the individual becoming more deeply aware of his or her experience of the world, and especially of other people, which translates into self-awareness and the nature of self in social context.

We think there is no more appropriate place to explore the paradoxes associated with social justice than the laboratory of higher education. First, it is the one institution in American society whose central mission is oriented toward pushing back the boundaries of knowledge in order to support an evolving democracy. Teaching and learning are necessarily evolutionary processes where static received knowledge is replaced with more differentiated and complex understandings of the world around us. Second, public higher education and the pursuit of knowledge need to be somewhat insulated from the whims and private interests of the marketplace in order to center both the "truth" and the common good. While we illustrated in Chapter Four that this insulation has worn dangerously thin, it is appropriate to ignite a shift back to the foundational *learning* purposes of higher education in order to move our democracy toward greater inclusion, fairness, and social justice. Insulation is important because it provides shelter for the kind of deep, critical, and controversial kinds of research and inquiry necessary to effectively explore new ideas and create new knowledge. It's a central reason why academic freedom policies were originally established. Third, most college students are at a prime meaning-making developmental level to begin shaking off the dogmas of passively received knowledge to initiate a self-authored, more fully mature sense of self and society that prepares them for full participation as citizens in our democracy.

Some readers may be looking for specific strategies that they can implement to effect change in higher education toward social justice. While we outlined a few particular approaches, developing social justice praxis demands a deeper internal shift than the language "technical strategies" implies. One can do more harm than good when one's social justice practice is either passively reflective or uncritically implemented. Social justice action is most effective when practice emerges from a deeply integrated sense of self in the world. Such practice reflexively tunes into context and history, applies a filter of critical pedagogy, maintains critical humility, listens compassionately, and consciously considers the ways in which our perspective at any time is limited.

Social justice practice that focuses only on the individual transcendence of prejudice and stereotypes is not enough. Critical capacities to interrogate institutional-level oppression—including how knowledge is constructed and maintained through forces of hegemony and power—are necessary, but not sufficient. The former fails to acknowledge systemic domination, while the latter leaves individual agency out of the discourse. While it is difficult to balance a focus on the institutional and the individual, it's what effective social justice practice demands. Similarly, we must find a way to reconcile the tensions between cognitive critique and human compassion. Educators need to know how to implement competencies emotionally as well as intellectually to work toward equal access to equity and justice for marginalized individuals and groups (Constantine, Hage, Kindaichi, & Bryant, 2007).

While wielding the sharp edges of critical theory or other forms of knowledge may make education professionals feel empowered and their practice more efficient, doing so can be much less effective. There is very little related to the nature of learning or the nature of social justice praxis that is efficient. In fact, efficiency is an artifact of the marketplace hegemony so endemic in today's culture. *Effectiveness* should be the rubric by which successful learning and social justice outcomes are measured, not efficiency. In this chapter, we will clarify and reinforce practices that emerge from the concepts discussed throughout the book and outline strategies for positioning social justice as part of the larger project of higher education reform currently underway.

Critical Counterhegemonic Practices

There is no substitute for carefully reading, deeply reflecting upon, and discussing the complexities related to social justice. Ideas like hegemony, dialectic, and discourse analysis are difficult to understand and even more difficult to apply. Unless one can conceptualize how reality is constructed and the dynamic forces at play, however, there can be no effective social justice praxis. Our experience is that using the concepts discussed in this book has provided a lens through which various forms of oppression, privilege, and other hurdles to social justice make sense. Moreover, by expanding our view beyond individual prejudices to include mechanisms through which oppression is maintained, we practice empathy for those with whom we may disagree. For example, when we consider hegemony, how knowledge is socially constructed, and how power maintains a limited ideology, it makes sense that we encounter people who espouse beliefs consistent with the dominant discourses. It is not surprising that the president of Chick-fil-A, for example, made comments about same-sex marriage that target gay people for oppression in stark contrast to principles of equity and justice (Aarthun, 2012). As we describe in Chapter Six, there are dominant antigay ideologies masquerading as objective reality that are legitimized by institutions like various churches and reinforced as "normal." The strategies one employs, however, knowing how such oppression is maintained and reinforced, should be congruent with how such knowledge is developed.

Counternarratives

Counterhegemony strategies do just that. According to Weiler (2009), counterhegemony is "a self-conscious analysis of a situation and the development of collective practices and organization that can oppose the hegemony of the existing order and begin to build the base for a new understanding and transformation of society" (p. 235). Such strategies interrupt oppression by illuminating hidden stories and provide more accurate depictions of reality. Harper's (2009; Harper & Davis, 2012) work provides an illustration of counterhegemony. Harper grew tired of reading titles in academic journals and news headlines that formed a deficit narrative regarding African American men. Harper (2009) illustrates how almost everything published about black male collegians negatively portrays them as underachieving and unlikely to succeed. The result is lowered expectations, higher dropout rates, and general disengagement, making an already oppressive institutional environment even worse. In reaction, Harper conducted the National Black Male College Achievement Study, the largest-ever empirical research study of black male undergraduates. He collected data from 219 successful students at 42 colleges and universities in 20 states across the United States. The counterstories Harper published stand in stark contrast to the deficit-informed master narrative, as men in his study describe successes, powerful resistance to racism they encountered on campus, and courageously overcoming oppression to take on leadership positions and thrive academically. Identity-based programming, therefore, may initially focus on providing safe harbor, but should move swiftly toward raising consciousness of the need for countering hegemony.

But one doesn't need to conduct research to provide space for counternarratives or other counterhegemony strategies. Student affairs professionals, faculty, and others involved in education can design interventions that focus on the stories of lived experience for those from underrepresented populations who develop latent and unarticulated resistance to the sexism, racism, and other forms of oppression they routinely encounter. As Giroux (1983) points out, the concept of resistance highlights the need for educators to "decipher how modes of cultural production displayed by subordinate groups can be analyzed to reveal both the limits and their possibilities for enabling critical thinking, analytic discourse, and new modes of intellectual appropriation" (p. 111). In the first paper for one of my courses on developmental theory, I (Davis) ask students to write their identity stories related to privilege and oppression. Students are later asked to interview students representing identities different from their own and compare these stories to the theories we read and their own experiences. In addition, students are encouraged to use resources related to history, like Takaki (1993) and Zinn (2005), as well as texts that give first-person accounts of a wide diversity of individuals typically left out of the master narrative like Bridwell-Bowles' (1998) *Identity Matters: Rhetorics of Difference* or Adams et al. (2010) *Readings for Diversity and Social Justice*. Another counterhegemony pedagogical strategy is to present contemporary stories of oppression and ask students to discover for themselves the reasons for them. One of our colleagues shows a one-page report that illustrates income distribution, racial demographics, and public school K–12 funding. Rather than lecturing about what his scholarly perspective is on the disparities, he uses this as a final exam for students to apply the concepts they have been learning throughout the course. Students thus participate in the construction of a critical perspective.

Similarly, service learning programs, residence life, Greek affairs, and other student affairs functional areas can offer programs that specifically highlight counternarratives and give voice to resistance. Service learning classes and trips can be particularly powerful sites for analyzing social justice where the realities of oppressed communities can be met with a conceptual framework to empower students toward transformation (Weigert & Crews, 1999). Such interventions need to go much deeper than food offerings or what we call the "click like" strategies too often used in education that leave systematic oppression, material disparities, and master narratives uninterrogated. The realities of hegemony can be taught, for example, by viewing the movie *The Matrix* (Silver, Wachowski, & Wachowski, 1999) and then comparing it to Plato's allegory of the cave. Power and ideology can be unveiled in nearly every content area by asking the following: Whose interests are represented? Whose voices are marginalized? What are other perspectives on this issue, and what does credible evidence suggest? How would history, positionality, or awareness of power and hegemony influence our understanding? Maintaining and modeling a critical perspective teaches students to develop a mindful self-authored narrative that is conscious of the sociological forces shaping them.

Dialectical Disposition

Maintaining a dialectical disposition for Freire (2000) is fundamentally a matter of building on our natural tendency toward curiosity. His work with those lacking formal education in Brazil taught him that the curiosity that scholars cultivate through methodological training is similar to the curiosity of those without educational privilege experience. In fact, he argues that a fundamental challenge for educators is to move students from what he calls "ingenious curiosity" to "epistemological curiosity," where understanding how knowledge is constructed and maintained empowers learners to develop critical thinking, consciousness about the world, and agency. Freire sees curiosity "as restless questioning, as movement toward the revelation of something hidden, as a question verbalized or not, as search for clarity, as a moment of attention, suggestion, and vigilance [that] constitutes an integral part of the phenomenon of being alive. There could be no creativity without the curiosity that moves us and sets us patiently impatient before a world that we did not make, to add to it something of our own making" (pp. 37–38). Counterhegemonic practice, as described here through counternarratives, dialectical questioning, and thoughtful implementation of critique, is more a "way of being" than the technical implementation of strategies. While readers may be looking for a more tangible set of approaches, as we've reinforced throughout this book, they cannot be handed over or passively bestowed. Learners must breathe life into the concepts and actively set about critiquing and making them their own.

Returning to the Chick-fil-A president's comments regarding same-sex marriage, we can apply the questions from the end of the last section. On July 2, Chick-fil-A president Don Cathy was interviewed by *Biblical Recorder*, an online journal for Baptists in North Carolina. During the interview Cathy affirmed that "We are very much supportive of the family—the biblical definition of the family unit. We are a family-owned business, a family-led business, and we are married to our first wives" (Blume, 2012, p. 1). The first question is: Whose interests are represented? It appears that Cathy is representing both the business interests of his company and his religion. The interests of those who believe heterosexuality is the only "moral" orientation also appear to be represented. Question 2: Whose voices are marginalized? Certainly the "biblical definition of the family unit" has been routinely used by those who are anti–gay marriage to claim authority for their beliefs, so making this statement places those who are gay in the margins. Question 3: What are other perspectives on this issue, and what does credible evidence suggest? There appear to be both support for and stances against the belief that the Bible defines a family unit as being based on heterosexual relationships. Regarding biblical evidence, gay marriage is not directly mentioned, although a handful of quotes can be lifted from context to suggest that sex between same-sex individuals is prohibited. Using the same strategy, however, biblical language can be taken to mandate the stoning to death of an alleged adulterer or, taken out of context, can seem to mandate the killing of one's children by smashing them against a rock (see Psalm 137:9). Thus, a "truth" that is based on biblical text may or may not be "God's word," but what we do in fact know is that biblical scholars have clearly established that "the Bible as we know it—or as I wish more people actually knew it—is more the work of editors than of authors. Moreover, it is the editorial work of human beings from different cultures, different eras, using different languages and subsets of the languages" (Cook, 2012, p. 1). In other words, while it is reasonable to believe that the Bible is "God's word" or the "truth," it is unreasonable to believe that our human interpretations of this text, especially given the many language translations it has received, are universal, much less accurate. Finally, Question 4: How would history, positionality, or awareness of power and hegemony influence our understanding? We will allow you, the reader, to fully answer this question, but clearly Cathy's position as a wealthy, white, Christian, able-bodied man in the United States who makes a public comment about an identity that is targeted for oppression is important. In addition, making this comment and getting wide attention in the media at a point in history when a contentious presidential campaign is under way can serve to solidify Christian and other voters who share Cathy's view. We welcome and in fact challenge readers to offer alternative perspectives to our construction of this issue.

We also believe the reader needs to decide—in social justice situations like the one just described, where equity and fairness are at risk—to take the side of those who have appropriated wealth, land, and the knowledge of the sociocultural system or those who have been targeted for oppression. As Aronowitz (2001) argues, "Freire judges current social and political arrangements by the criterion of whether they have taken steps to ameliorate, much less reverse, the long tradition of authoritarian societies to exclude substantial portions of their populations from participation in economic, social, and cultural life and whether they further or retard humanity's project of self-fulfillment" (p. 11). While combining critical reflection with a methodology that seeks to uncover generally hidden influences like power and hegemony is essential, it should be implemented not in some apolitical, disinterested, or seemingly objective way, but actually in an ideological manner. To use critical pedagogy and other counterhegemony strategies is to take a decidedly transparent political stand in favor of the disenfranchised and against liberty-limiting policies, practices, and procedures. Taking an overtly political stand also comes with the responsibility to behave in manners congruent with civil discourse and, when challenging laws, following tenets of civil disobedience. Resistance that inspires violence or shuts down dialogue is antithetical to the social justice practice we espouse.

In a culture that mistakes certainty for insight and consistency for integrity, it is difficult to maintain a dialectical disposition. Politicians, for example, in many national campaigns we have witnessed claim that their opponent is a "flip-flopper," as if someone should be born with all the knowledge necessary to maintain the ideas they held earlier in life or as if context, history, or new knowledge should not affect emerging perspectives. One may lack integrity if what he or she says to different audiences is different, but it is not a threat to integrity to have an open mind that shifts perspective in response to new evidence. In fact, it lacks integrity to do otherwise. This form of dialectical practice stands in stark contrast to many traditional ways of promoting student learning. Many educators and student affairs professionals behave in ways that reinforce certainty, promote conformity, and advocate technical control of knowledge. Engaging in dialectical discourse focuses in on the relationship between individual and society and between objectivity and subjectivity. It acknowledges that our view of the world is necessarily incomplete, and movement toward greater clarity comes from the awareness of how our position both limits and captures phenomena. To be dialectical requires one to always remain open to the possibility of new knowledge, unseen influences, and hidden relationships.

Critical Humility and Compassionate Listening

If applying a cognitive-instrumental rationality alone were effective in bringing about social justice, we would fully support it. The reality is that cognitive understanding and individual consciousness do not necessarily translate into effecting individual growth or institutional change. As important as intellectual understanding of the philosophical framework we've outlined in this book is (for example, hegemony, social construction of knowledge, attention to context and history, and power), the processes one uses to effect change need to be met with an equally sophisticated set of interpersonal and intrapersonal skills. While there is a wide variety of competencies that influence the effective delivery of education interventions and the promotion of social justice, we believe the most important intrapersonal skill is critical humility and the chief interpersonal skill is compassionate listening.

Critical humility embodies a delicate and demanding balance of speaking out for social justice while at the same time remaining aware that our knowledge is partial and evolving (Barlas et al., 2010). This is very similar to Freire's (2000) articulation of the human condition being synonymous with being unfinished. Our awareness of our own "unfinishedness" is central to critical humility. It requires that we not only maintain consciousness that we still have more to learn, but openness to considering other possibilities. Behaviors reflecting such practice include listening and questioning, rather than asserting and debating. This is much more difficult than it seems, particularly when we are discussing the controversial or sensitive topics that are generally involved in social justice practice. Barlas et al., for example, say that "over our years of working together, we have struggled to stay in an inquiry mode that avoids the smug sense of confidence that we have 'done the work' and therefore achieved the 'right' perceptions about Whiteness, race, and dominating systems of power" (2010, p. 155). They go on to identify typical behaviors they have used when they forget that they are unfinished. One is proselytizing, which they define as "exhorting in an officious and tiresome way," and the other is disdaining, or "treating as less worthy and rejecting with aloof contempt or scorn" (p. 146). According to Barlas et al., these behaviors arise in part from a desire to both be and be seen as good social justice advocates or, in terms of race, to be seen as "good" white people. This shifts attention our from critical humility to a desire to be "superior to other White people who 'just don't get it' ... [and] in our zeal to enlighten them, we end up proselytizing in ways that put them on the defensive or close down conversation altogether (Barlas et al., 2010, p. 146). In our denial of being similarly positioned and wanting to distance ourselves from both the privileges received and oppression perpetuated by systemic racism or other form of oppression, we make others feel defensive or patronized.

As Barlas et al. (2010) work toward building capacity to embody critical humility, they have found the following questions helpful in constructing communication strategies that promote openness rather than defensiveness:

    a. *Self-Identity and Values.* What is the identity label I seek to avoid? How do I see myself as different from others in this situation?

    b. *Role of Privilege.* What privilege is operating in this situation? Acknowledging that we all have multiple identities, which ones are salient here? In what ways am I resisting perceiving myself as in a dominant position?

    c. *Purpose.* How might I be perpetuating the phenomenon I wish to change in this situation?

    d. *Self-Reflective Process.* To what extent have I disclosed myself, allowed myself to be vulnerable to new learning? How am I similar to that which I am criticizing? How is my information incomplete? [pp. 150–152].

I (Davis) have personally worn the mask of being finished. When I've done so, it came from the need to be seen as having expertise (for example, ego), to justify my credentials, or to deny my generally privileged positionality. I have seen, upon reflection, how such masking not only subverts authenticity, but also distances me from those I am trying to engage in social justice discourse and ironically subverts my goal.

In addition to critical humility, we have learned that compassionate listening is one of the most central skills in promoting learning and a social justice disposition in students. Like critical humility, listening with compassion requires a focus, paradoxically, both on self and away from self. According to Garrison (2010), "we care for others best when we care for ourselves, but to care for ourselves well, we must care for others. To maintain such a precarious balance requires that we avoid the extremes of self-eradication and egotistic self-assertion in favor of what I call self-eclipse" (p. 2764). Ego-centered self-assertion seeks power over others, and self-eradication acquiesces all power to others. Self-eclipse, on the other hand, helps us suspend our dogmas of received knowledge and impassioned habits of proselytizing in order to focus simultaneously on self and other, on personal and institutional, and to listen deeply before we construct our own answers. Too often in higher education, we construct a debate-style response out of our received knowledge in our ego-centered attempt to be right, rather than seeking understanding. Garrison challenges us to practice compassionate listening, which offers "hospitality to the differences of others instead of reducing everything and everyone to the sameness of a predetermined mode. Such beings will not eradicate the identity of others, nor will they allow others to eradicate their own identity. They grasp the following paradox of learning: To grow, we must learn about others, while to learn about others, we must learn about ourselves" (2010, p. 2764). We have found that focused listening is actually more difficult than talking or constructing a response. To receive, clarify, and understand is both inefficient and effective. The kind of listening we advocate here emerges from genuine curiosity about the other, receives the pain or suffering that someone else has experienced, but responds with sympathy, not pity. We also have found that compassionate listening in and of itself can be transformative. It may be counterintuitive to believe that what appears to be passive listening can be more transformative than something said or done. Such listening, however, allows for the activation of self-authorship and in our experience provides a sort of canvas upon which students can paint their experiences to more clearly see how they have constructed knowledge. We've found listening such an important aspect of classroom discussion that we have compiled a list of common group norms in Exhibit 8.1 that we encourage groups and classes to consider establishing to encourage compassionate listening and deeper learning.

Exhibit 8.1. Common Group Norms to Enhance Social Justice Discourse

- Really listen—don't talk over others
- Take risks, lean into the discomfort
- Speak from personal experience: use "I" statements to share thoughts and feelings
- Treat each other with respect
- Be fully present
- Ask clarifying questions when you don't understand
- Notice and name group dynamics in the moment
- Agree to disagree
- Consider how and why you've gotten where you are today
- Participate fully (at your own comfort level)
- Take responsibility for the group
- Keep confidentiality—which is expected, but not guaranteed—to create safe space

(continued)

(continued)

- Self-attribute your motives and thoughts; do not assume about others
- Respect that we are all at different places
- Be aware that everyone has a story that is important

In addition to this list, we have used Palmer's (2004) conception of the Quaker circle or the circle of trust as a strategy for creating the kind of learning community where multiple perspectives are respected and differences explored. In a circle of trust, the focus is on providing space for seeking truth that embodies compassionate listening rather than advice giving, speaking our own truths rather than setting someone else straight, and asking honest questions instead of imparting answers. Palmer advocates using metaphors, poems, music, stories, or other artistic media that intentionally raise an important topic, but do so in a manner that promotes a balancing of the object of discussion with the subjects in the room. Mediated by what he calls this "third thing, truth can emerge from, and return to, our awareness at whatever pace and depth we are able to handle—sometimes inwardly in silence, sometimes aloud in community—giving the shy soul the protective cover it needs" (p. 92). We have similarly used a strategy offered by Nash (2001) in which he challenges us to engage in moral conversation where we see the truth in that which we disagree with and the error in our own perspective as we enter into discussion. The key here is to create contexts that inhibit our tendency toward argument and debate that carts out received dogma in order to instead deeply listen to those with whom we disagree. A test to the success of such strategies, then, is our dispositional receptivity to ideas we find offensive. It also means we can't invoke "safe space" arguments every time someone says something we don't like. Social justice–oriented discussions must be balanced by sensitivities to difference on the one hand and an obligation to receive what we might find offensive on the other—a sort of midpoint between liberty and responsibility.

Matching Learner Meaning-Making Capacity with Effective Learning Strategies

So far we have explored the necessity of balancing cognition (for example, critical critique), interpersonal issues (for example, listening), and intrapersonal skills (for example, ego management) for effective implementation of transformative learning and social justice practice. We've argued that social justice practice that raises consciousness and challenges systems of oppression is not simply an intellectual process, but as Kegan (1982, 1994) illustrates, a mix of intellectual, interpersonal, and intrapersonal meaning making. Moving individuals to a place where they comprehend some of the complexities necessary for doing effective social justice practice takes patience by teachers and an understanding of the ways to be "good company" along the way. As Kegan (1994) points out, "Multiselved postmodern parents do not mate and give birth to multiselved postmodern babies. Half a lifetime, if not more, precedes these discoveries ... and good company is required every step of the way" (p. 331). Rather than becoming annoyed or worse, Kegan has found a way to empathize with those who resist the kind of conceptualization necessary for effective social justice practice and transform frustration into one of connection. He offers, in fact, practical strategies that appropriately meet learners' meaning-making capacity to challenge them to become more critical and move into a more self-authored position.

In his description of learner positions and corresponding facilitative environments (or the way education professionals should respond), Kegan (1982, 1994) suggests that we meet the psychological position of defending with confirmation. Consider students' use of the term *gay* to mean "dumb" or "stupid." If this student has learned from her peers and others that this is an appropriate use of the word *gay*, then it makes sense that she would defend her use of the term in this manner. Rather than assuming the student is being pejorative and challenging with arguments about oppression or telling them not to use the term in this manner, educators should meet this behavior with confirmation. Asking a question, for example, about what they believe the term means is consistent with confirmation. According to the model described in Table 8.1, we are not confirming the appropriateness of the term; to the contrary, the ultimate aim is to disrupt oppression and promote learning. We are confirming that it makes sense and is reasonable that someone would learn to use the term in an inappropriate manner and it's valid to feel some confusion and a desire to defend. Moreover, confirmation is the first step in a three-step process that includes contradiction and continuity. While it is also reasonable for educators to want to punish someone whose behavior supports oppression, we have a professional responsibility to promote learning (and social justice) through methods that open up, not shut down, learning opportunities. Admonishing conduct we think is oppressive may make us feel better, but it can also suppress learning. According to Kegan, confirmation can take the form of identifying commonalities with the student, establishing and modeling ground rules for respectful listening, affirming that it's okay to be uninformed and confused, and identifying misinformation, stereotypes, or assumptions. Essentially, ignorance and potentially oppressive behavior are met with the creation of a safe environment where defenses are more permeable. An understanding of students' development should help educational professionals further understand the need to meet potentially oppressive statements first with a strategy of confirmation. Community members feeling confirmed and understood are more likely to express emotions like confusion and fear. Once confirmation is used, students are more likely to surrender dogmatic positions, paving the way for subsequent strategies related to further growth (Kegan, 1982, 1994). In contradiction, for example, professionals can explore how the student's use of

Table 8.1. Kegan's Learning Positions, Corresponding Facilitative Environments, and Bell and Griffin's Strategies to Achieve Growth

Learning Position	Facilitative Response	Learning Strategies
Defending The way things are (what we've learned); we defend this worldview from threats of new information	*Confirmation* Feelings of confusion and anger are confirmed, and a safe environment is constructed that makes defenses more permeable	Establish and model ground rules of respectful listening Identify misinformation, stereotypes, and assumptions Affirm that it's okay to be uninformed and confused Use low-risk self-disclosure activities early to establish norm of interaction, reflection, disclosure
Surrendering Of passively received dogmas and knowledge to begin a liberating exploration toward constructing self-authorship	*Contradiction* Immersion in contradictions, posing and exploring paradoxes, feelings of frustration and anger are a necessary part of this process as some feel betrayed at learning how knowledge has been constructed, sold, and maintained	Validate personal risk taking Encourage full discussion with multiple perspectives Allow contradictions to emerge and resist temptation to smother Guided imagery
Reintegration Of old foundation with new; the past is not rejected, but rather reinterpreted	*Continuity* Help confirm new learning, facilitate constructing action plans that reflect new ideas, explore how to behave in old contexts with new perspectives	Identify wide variety of action possibilities Identify ways to find support for standing up to actions against social justice Summarize and initiate closure

the term is different from your understanding and begin to "be good company" in exploring how that language was sold and how it is paradoxically constructed. Table 8.1 lists learner positions, corresponding facilitative environments, and specific strategies suggested by Bell and Griffin (1997) to encourage movement to a more complex, self-authored way of making meaning necessary for effective social justice practice.

Growth-inducing dialogue and social justice–oriented practice, furthermore, should sequence learning interventions that move from low to high risk, from concrete to abstract concepts, from personal experience to institutional forces, from difference to dominance, and from "what" to "so what" to "now what" (Bell & Griffin, 1997). A central reason for illustrating these learning processes, not just content, is that effectively implementing social justice practice demands it. Many in higher education naively behave as if students bring only their brains to campus and our only goal is to have them think more complexly. We argue that this is not congruent with the way students experience learning, the goals of higher education, and the societal demand that we promote the development of engaged democratic citizens. Evidence clearly suggests that we need to bring our whole selves to social justice praxis that invites others to also be fully human. If linear, forceful methods were effective, we would actively advocate their use. However, people learn and grow when they're given space to be vulnerable, are confirmed when they feel exposed, and are supported through the contradictions that critical pedagogical practices will activate.

Social Justice Allies

Both dominant and targeted individuals are affected by systems of oppression, and it is the goal of social justice education to liberate people from both internalized dominance and internalized oppression. At its most fundamental level, our humanness demands authenticity. Hosting oppression or dominance subjects our experience of self to the myths constructed by externally authored master narratives. In contrast, we believe in promoting the freedom for learners to construct their identities by picking and choosing for themselves the beliefs that provide meaning and direction to their lives. The process for becoming liberated from oppression is outlined by Fanon (2008) and others. It has only been in the last few decades that scholarship focused attention on privilege and those who hold dominant identities in any given culture (for example, Adams, Bell, & Griffin, 2007; Broido, 2000; Edwards, 2006; Fabiano et al., 2003; Goodman, 2000; Johnson, 2006; Kendall, 2006; McIntosh, 1988; Reason, Broido, Davis & Evans, 2005). We agree with hooks (2004), who writes, "After hundreds of years of anti-racist struggle, more than ever before non-white people are currently calling attention to the primary role white people must play in anti-racist struggle. The same is true of the struggle to eradicate sexism—men have a primary role to play" (p. 559). Moreover, Johnson (2006) writes, "the simple truth is that (injustice) can't be solved unless people who are heterosexual or male or Anglo or White or economically comfortable feel obligated to make the problem of privilege their problem and do something about it" (p. 10).

People aware of how privilege operates to create internalized dominance and who are committed to working to dismantle systems of oppression are sometimes called social justice allies. A social justice ally is someone from a dominant social group who is "working to end the system of oppression that gives them greater privilege and power based on their social-group membership" (Broido, 2000, p. 3). Becoming a social justice ally is no easy task and incorporates many of the complexities we've already outlined throughout this book. Exhibit 8.2 illustrates the self-understanding, actions, institutional change strategies, and the ways to support target group members that are characteristic of social justice allies.

Exhibit 8.2. Becoming a Social Justice Ally: Summary from Reason, Broido, Davis, and Evans (2005)

A. Self-understanding

- Continue to read about issues of social justice, building an understanding of power, privilege, oppression.

- Identify the multiple identities you possess, recognizing their interaction, the ways in which those identities may shift over your lifetime, and how their meaning may shift depending on context.

- Critically examine the role of your power, privilege, and oppression in your daily life, moving these three abstractions into concrete understandings.

- Avoid impulsive actions in favor of actions based on reflection, contemplation, and compassion, avoiding the "guilty liberal" impulse to action (Dass & Gorman, 1985; Tatum, 1997).

- Take time to struggle through the inevitable cognitive and affective dissonance created when good people recognize the realities of living within societal structures that reinforce inequality.

- Recognize and weigh the consequences (positive and negative) you may encounter in assuming a social justice ally identity. Are the possible positive outcomes worth the difficulties you may face?

- Be able to articulate why you do this work. What motivates you? How does this work fit with your own values, spiritual beliefs, and life purposes?

- Identify your own benefit in doing this work. Having a clear understanding of how your life would be better in the absence of oppression will help you withstand challenges to the work. Bowser and Hunt's *The Impact of Racism on White Americans* (1996), while specific to racism, is an excellent resource on this topic.

- Know your own strengths and limits. Some of us are gifted teachers but less comfortable in more politicized situations. Some of us excel at organizing large groups of people; some of us can communicate in ways that are heard well by those with formal power. Few of us are equally effective in all arenas; knowing our talents will maximize our ability to create social change.

B. Ally actions

- Engage with dominant group members in discussions about power, privilege, and oppressions of all types, even when such discussion may make others less comfortable. Incorporate those discussions into all facets of your work; social justice issues arise as much in talking about budget priorities as in programs focused specifically on oppression.

- Recognize and point out instances of power and privilege differentials during interactions with others. Do so to raise awareness.

- Study the history of social justice movements and the roles of dominant group members in those histories (Kivel, 2002). Talk with other dominant group members about what you learn. Challenge the myth that dominant group members cannot effect change.

- Confront inappropriate comments and behaviors in ways that educate rather than demean or embarrass.

- Develop confrontation skills that alleviate defensive reactions from other dominant group members. Johnson's book *Power, privilege, and difference* (2006) is a wonderful resource to assist in this endeavor.

- Create environments where ally behavior is expected. Incorporate expectations of ally behavior into guidelines for resident assistants, peer educators, orientation leaders, and other student leadership roles.

- Explicitly invite students into ally behavior by asking them to join you and other students in ally actions.

- Persevere. Overcome initial defensiveness of dominant group members through prolonged engagement.

C. Creating institutional and cultural change

- Support the recruitment and retention of diverse students, faculty, and staff. While most researchers have concluded that structural diversity is insufficient to enhance learning, it is necessary to create the diverse interpersonal interactions necessary for learning.

- Study and improve campus climates. One must feel safe in order to learn and grow.

- Advocate for social justice course work. If social justice courses are not currently available, advocate for their development; if courses exist, encourage students to enroll in them. Nothing indicates institutional

(continued)

(continued)

support on a college campus more than including the curriculum as a for-credit course.

- Advocate for inclusion of social justice issues across the curriculum and cocurriculum. Specific social justice courses are not enough; a social justice perspective should permeate the campus climate.

- Work to change unjust policies, practices, and laws. Identify where groups are treated unjustly (for example, lack of partner benefits for lesbian and gay employees), and lobby for change. Expand your influence beyond campus to local, state, and federal governments.

- Know and use institutional decision-making structures strategically (von Destinon, Evans, & Wall, 2000). Student and faculty groups often have considerable power to enact change and can serve as partners in change.

- Frequent institutions that support justice; boycott institutions that do not. Educate others about both types of institutions.

- Persevere. Institutional change occurs slowly, but that must not dissuade action.

D. Supporting target group members

- Listen. Do not assume you are an expert (Kivel, 2002). No matter how long you have been an ally, you have much to learn from members of target groups.

- Diversify your friendship group. Make a point to develop relationships with people who are visibly (and invisibly) different from you. Then be a friend.

- Be visible in your support, being careful that your visibility does not take attention away from target group members. Be visible to and with target group members, not in lieu of them.

- Educate yourself so that you can effectively provide support to target group members. Know the history of target group members, as well as institutional, local, and national resources available to assist and support them.

- Do not expect praise. Target group members may be ambivalent about your support at first (Bishop, 2002).

- Apologize when necessary (von Destinon, Evans, & Wall, 2000). Allies make mistakes; effective allies recognize their mistakes, apologize, and learn from them.
- Persevere. Giving up when the situation becomes difficult sends a message of wavering support to target group members and reinforces a sense of distrust between groups.

Working toward becoming a social justice ally can be treacherous but very rewarding work. Our experience in observing social justice ally development is that those making this journey sometimes lose friends along the way, experience significant family turmoil, feel at risk for supervisor retaliation, and are sometimes accused of being traitors. Rewards, however, can include movement toward self-authorship, integrity, self-respect that comes from acting on the courage of your convictions, and the soul-deep connection with others who similarly are working together to interrupt oppression and promote social justice.

Conclusion

We have deeply grounded faith that students and others in higher education will listen to the voices of those we've cited throughout this book (and upon whose shoulders we stand) to more clearly see why we are not closer than we are to realizing a more socially just democracy. We believe that there are many who are willing to work to combat the commodification efforts by market forces currently subverting the purposes of higher education described in Chapter Three. *New York Times* reporter M. S. Handler (1992), states that "thirty years of experience as a reporter in Western and Eastern Europe had taught me that the forces in a developing social struggle are frequently buried beneath the visible surface and make themselves felt in many ways long before they burst out into the open" (viii). There is evidence, like the Occupy Movement, the widest income disparity since the Great Depression, and campus protests in response to sexism, racism, and homophobia, that people are frustrated. We agree with Handler, who further argues that "these generative forces make themselves felt through the power of an idea long before their organizational forms can openly challenge the establishment.... In the United States, it is our weakness to confuse the numerical strength of an organization and the publicity attached to leaders with the germinating forces that sow the seeds of social upheaval in our community" (1992, p. viii). We hope the ideas humbly offered in this book provide readers such a germinating force—that you will develop social justice praxis that is mindful of the concepts we've presented and educators we've cited.

Such a movement will require the kind of unity described by Baszile (2005): "The concept of unity is complicated; it no longer indicates a state of sameness and absolute agreement; rather it becomes the process of constantly working toward a united front in light of difference. Thus any group of diverse people engaged in a struggle for power through representation needs not only to understand the significance of a united front, but also needs to interrogate their visions of unity" (p. 142). Consistent with the recursive demands of critical theory, then, any sense of unity and common cause needs to remain open to challenges. The processes associated with maintaining such a stance are related to what we call Social Justice 2.0 in the Preface and have described in subsequent chapters. To move beyond a social justice paradigm that either emerges simply out of a desire for "positive diversity" or one that positions those with privilege outside of the movement, we need to embrace ambiguity, unrest, and disruption. As Baszile argues, "teachable moments are precisely when public performances go awry; it is only in the context of these disrupted performances that critical questions about those everyday ways of acting, thinking, being on stage can be questioned and challenged" (2005, p. 146). Such moments offer opportunities to expose epistemological frameworks that maintain oppression. When we develop effective methods for embracing such disruptive performances in higher education, it requires balancing our anger with compassion, critical mindfulness with humble awareness of being unfinished, and listening others into voice rather than shouting them down. Implementing Social Justice 2.0 can move us beyond static educational practices that don't seem to be creating change. Fundamentally, such effective praxis needs to focus on illuminating epistemological frameworks that both maintain the status quo and offer liberatory strategies toward social justice.

References

Aarthun, S. (2012, July 27). How the Chick-fil-A same-sex marriage controversy has evolved. *CNN news*. Retrieved from http://news.blogs.cnn.com /2012/07/27/how-the-chick-fil-a-same-sex-marriage-controversy-has-evolved

Abes, E. S., Jones, S. R., & McEwen, M. K. (2007). Reconceptualizing the model of multiple dimensions of identity: The role of meaning-making capacity in the construction of multiple identities. *Journal of College Student Development*, 48, 1–21.

Ada, A. F., & Beutel, C. M. (1993). *Participatory research as a dialogue for social action*. Unpublished manuscript.

Adams, G., & Balfour, D. (2009). *Unmasking administrative evil*. London: M. E. Sharpe.

Adams, J. Q. (2003; Contributing Ed.). In J. W. Collins III & N. P. O'Brien (Eds.), *The Greenwood dictionary of education*. Westport, CT: Greenwood Press.

Adams, M., Bell, L. A., & Griffin, P. (1997). *Teaching for diversity and social justice: A sourcebook for teachers and trainers*. New York: Routledge.

Adams, M., Bell, L. A., & Griffin, P. (2007). *Teaching for diversity and social justice* (2nd ed.). New York: Routledge.

Adams, M., Blumenfeld, W. J., Castaneda, C., Hackman, H. W., Peters, M. L., & Zuniga, X. (Eds.). (2010). *Readings for diversity and social justice:*

An anthology on racism, antisemitism, sexism, heterosexism, ableism, and classism.
New York: Routledge.

Adelman, L. (Producer), & Herbes-Sommers, C. (Director). (2003). *Race: The power of an illusion* [Documentary film]. United States: California Newsreel.

Ali, S. R., & Bagheri, E. (2005). Practical suggestions to accommodate the needs of Muslim students on campus. In S. K. Watt, E. E. Fairchild, & K. M. Goodman (Eds.), *Intersections of religious privilege: Difficult dialogues and student affairs practice* (pp. 47–54). New Directions for Student Services, No. 125. San Francisco: Jossey-Bass.

Alvarez, J. (2009). Foreword: Rapunzel's ladder social justice education: A way down from the ivory tower. In K. Skubikowski, C. Wright, & R. Graf (Eds.), *Social justice education: Inviting faculty to transform their institutions* (pp. xiii–xiv). Sterling, VA: Stylus.

Alvesson, M., Bridgman, T., & Willmott, H. (Eds.). (2011). *The Oxford handbook of critical management studies* (pp. 1–26). Oxford: Oxford University Press.

American Council on Education. (2002). *Making the case for affirmative action in higher education: On the importance of diversity in higher education.* Washington, DC: Author.

American Council on Education. (2011). *Status report on minorities in higher education.* Washington, DC: Author.

Aronowitz, S. (2001). Introduction. In P. Freire (Author), *Pedagogy of freedom: Ethics, democracy, and civic courage* (pp. 1–19). Lanham, MD: Rowman & Littlefield.

Arum, R. (2011). *Academically adrift: Limited learning on college campuses.* Chicago: University of Chicago Press.

Astin, A. W. (1993). *What matters in college? Four critical years revisited.* San Francisco: Jossey-Bass.

Badaracco, J. (2002). *Leading quietly: An unorthodox guide to doing the right thing.* Boston: Harvard Business School Press.

Bailey, M. J., & Dynarski, S. M. (2011). Inequality in postsecondary education. In G. J. Duncan & R. Murnane (Eds.), *Whither opportunity: Rising inequality, schools, and children's life chances* (pp. 117–132). New York: Russell Sage Foundation.

Bain, K. (2004). *What the best college teachers do.* Cambridge, MA: Harvard University Press.

Barber, B. (1995, March–April). The search for civil society. In *Rebuilding Civil Society: A symposium from The New Democrat, 7*(2). Retrieved from http://www.cpn.org/parties/search.html

Barlas, C., Kasl, E., MacLeod, A., Paxton, D. Rosenwasser, P., & Sartor, L. (2010). White on white: Developing capacity to communicate about race with critical humility. In V. Sheared, J. Johnson-Bailey, S. Colin, E. Peterson, S. Brookfield, & Assoc. (Eds.), *The handbook of race and adult education* (pp. 145–157). San Francisco: Jossey-Bass.

Barlett, D., & Steele, J. (1998, November 9). Corporate welfare. *Time, 152*(19). Retrieved from http://www.time.com/time/magazine/article/0,9171,989508,00.html

Basler, R. P. (Ed.). (1953). *The collected works of Abraham Lincoln.* Volume 2. Springfield, IL: Abraham Lincoln Association. Retrieved from http://quod.lib.umich.edu/l/lincoln

Baszile, D. T. (2005). When public performances go awry: Reading the dynamics of diversity through power, pedagogy, and protest on campus. In B. K. Alexander, G. L. Anderson, & B. P. Gallegos (Eds.), *Performance theories in education: Power, pedagogy, and the politics of identity* (pp. 127–147). Mahwah, NJ: Erlbaum.

Bateson, G. (1991). *A sacred unity: Further steps to an ecology of mind.* New York: HarperCollins.

Bell, L. A. (2007). Theoretical foundations for social justice education. In M. Adams, L. A. Bell, & P. Griffin (Eds.), *Teaching for diversity and social justice* (pp. 1–14). New York: Routledge.

Bell, L. A., & Griffin, P. (1997). Designing social justice education courses. In M. Adams, L. A. Bell, & P. Griffin (Eds.), *Teaching for diversity and social justice: A sourcebook for teachers and trainers* (pp. 67–87). New York: Routledge.

Bell, L., Washington, S., Weinstein, G., & Love, B. (2003). Knowing ourselves as instructors. In A. Darder, M. Baltodano, & R. Torres (Eds.), *The critical pedagogy reader* (pp. 464–478). New York: RoutledgeFalmer.

Berger, P. (1966). *The social construction of reality: A treatise in the sociology of knowledge*. Garden City, NY: Doubleday.

Bertrand, M., & Mullainathan, B. (2004). Are Emily and Greg more employable than Lakisha and Jamal? A field experiment on labor market discrimination. *The American Economic Review, 94*(4), 991–1013.

Bickel, R. D. (1998). A brief history of the commitment to inclusion as a facet of equal educational opportunity. In D. D. Gehring (Ed.), *Responding to the new affirmative action climate* (pp. 3–13). San Francisco: Jossey-Bass.

Bishop, A. (2002). *Becoming an ally: Breaking the cycle of oppression in people*. London: Zed Books.

Blume, A. K. (2012, July 2). "Guilty as charged," Dan Cathy says of Chick-fil-A's stand on faith. *Biblical Recorder*. Retrieved from http://www.brnow.org /News/July-2012/%E2%80%98Guilty-as-charged,%E2%80%99-Dan-Cathy-says -of-Chick-fil-A

Blume, G. H., & Long, M. C. (2012). *Changes in affirmative action in the era of Hopwood, Grutter, and Gratz*. (Working Paper No. 2012–01). Seattle: University of Washington, Evans School of Public Affairs.

Bok, D. (2003). *Universities in the marketplace: The commercialization of higher education*. Princeton, NJ: Princeton University Press.

Bolte, C. G., & Harris, L. (1947). *Our negro veterans* (Pamphlet No. 128). New York: Public Affairs Committee.

Bowen, W., & Bok, D. (1998). *The shape of the river*. Princeton, NJ: Princeton University Press.

Bowser, B. P., & Hunt, R. G. (1996). *The impact of racism on white Americans.* Thousand Oaks, CA: Sage.

Brewis, J., & Jack, G. (2011). Culture: Broadening the critical repertoire. In M. Alvesson, T. Bridgeman, & H. Willmont (Eds.), *The Oxford handbook of critical management studies* (pp. 232–250). New York: Oxford University Press.

Bridwell-Bowles, L. (Ed.). (1998). *Identity matters: Rhetorics of difference.* Upper Saddle River, NJ: Prentice-Hall.

Broido, E. M. (2000). The development of social justice allies during college: A phenomenological investigation. *Journal of College Student Development, 41,* 3–17.

Brookfield, S. D. (2005). *The power of critical theory: Liberating adult learning and teaching.* San Francisco: Jossey-Bass.

Brown, B. (2010). *The gifts of imperfection: Let go of who you think you're supposed to be and embrace who you are.* Center City, MN: Hazelden.

Brown, G., Langer, A., & Stewart, F. (Eds.). (2012). *Affirmative action in plural societies.* New York: Palgrave Macmillan.

Brown v. Board of Education, 347 U.S. 483 (1954).

Buber, M. (1996). *I and thou.* New York: Touchstone.

Bush, J. (1999). Executive Order 99–281. Florida Department of Management Services. Retrieved from http://www.dms.myflorida.com/media/general_counsel_files/one_florida_executive_order_pdf

Byrd, C., Reed, W., & Graves, E. (2011, September 25). Class-based policies are not a remedy for racial inequality. *Chronicle of Higher Education, 58*(6), B35–B37.

Cahn, S. M. (1997, January–February). Two concepts of affirmative action. *Academe,* pp. 14–19.

Caputi, J. (2003). Everyday pornography. In G. Dines & J. McMahon Humez (Eds.), *Gender, race, and class in media: A text-reader* (pp. 434–450). Thousand Oaks, CA: Sage.

Carney, C. M. (1999). *Native American higher education in the United States.* New Brunswick, N.J.: Transaction.

Cass, V. C. (1979). Homosexual identity formation: A theoretical model. *Journal of Homosexuality, 4,* 219–235.

Chang, M. J., Astin, A. W., & Kim, D. (2004). Cross-racial interaction among undergraduates: Some consequences, causes, and patterns. *Research in Higher Education, 45*(5), 529–553.

Chang, M. J., Denson, N., Saenz, V., & Misa, K. (2006). The educational benefits of sustaining cross-racial interaction among undergraduates. *The Journal of Higher Education, 77,* 430–455.

Child, J. (2011). Challenging hierarchy. In M. Alvesson, T. Bridgman, & H. Willmott (Eds.), *The Oxford handbook of critical management studies* (pp. 501–514). Oxford: Oxford University Press.

Chizhik, E. W., & Chizhik, A. W. (2002). What do privilege and oppression really mean? *Journal of College Student Development, 43,* 792–808.

Chomsky, N. (2002). *Media control.* New York: Seven Stories Press.

Chomsky, N. (2003). *Hegemony or survival: America's quest for global dominance.* New York: Metropolitan Books.

Constantine, M. G., Hage, S. M., Kindaichi, M. M., & Bryant, R. M. (2007). Social justice and multicultural issues: Implications for the practice and training of counselors and counseling psychologists. *Cultural Diversity and Ethnic Minority Psychology, 11,* 162–175.

Cook, H. T. (2012, August 9). Guest commentary: Chick-fil-A president needs a taste of biblical history. *Detroit Free Press,* p. 5.

Coomes, M. D., & DeBard, R. (Eds.). (2004). *Serving the millennial generation*. San Francisco: Jossey-Bass.

Crenshaw, K. (1989). Demarginalizing the intersection of race and sex: A black feminist critique of antidiscrimination doctrine, feminist theory, and antiracist politics. *University of Chicago Legal Forum*, pp. *139–167*.

Crenshaw, K. (1991). Mapping the margins: Intersectionality, identity politics, and violence against women of color. *Stanford Law Review, 43*(6), 1241–1279.

Cross, W. E., Jr. (1995). The psychology of Nigrescence: Revisiting the Cross model. In J. G. Ponterotto, J. M. Casas, L. A. Suzuki, & C. M. Alexander (Eds.), *Handbook of multicultural counseling* (pp. 93–122). Thousand Oaks, CA: Sage.

Darder, A., Baltodano, M. P., & Torres, R. D. (Eds.). (2009). *The critical pedagogy reader* (2nd ed.). New York: Routledge.

Dass, R., & Gorman, P. (1985). *How can I help? Stories and reflections on service.* New York: Random House.

D'Augelli, A. R. (1994). Identity development and sexual orientation: Toward a model of lesbian, gay, and bisexual development. In E. J. Trickett, R. J. Watts, & D. Birman (Eds.), *Human diversity: Perspectives on people in context* (pp. 312–333). San Francisco: Jossey-Bass.

Davis, T. (2002). Voices of gender role conflict: The social construction of college men's identity. *Journal of College Student Development, 43*(4), 508–521.

Davis, T., Thomas, A., & Sewalish, C. (2006). Exploring the constructions of masculine identities among St. Lucian men. *Journal of Men's Studies, 14*(3), 292–310.

Decety, J., & Jackson, P. (2004). The functional architecture of human empathy. *Behavioral and Cognitive Neuroscience Reviews, 3*, 271–100. Retrieved from http://home.uchicago.edu/%7Edecety/publications/Decety_CDPS06.pdf

Destinon, M. von, Evans, N. J., & Wall, V. A. (2000). Navigating the minefield: Sexual orientation issues and campus politics. In N. J. Evans &

V. A. Wall (Eds.), *Toward acceptance: Sexual orientation issues on campus* (pp. 371–386). Lanham, MD: University Press of America.

Dill, B. & Zambrana, R. (2009). *Emerging intersections: Race, class, and gender in theory, policy and practice.* New Brunswick, NJ: Rutgers University Press.

Dilley, P. (2002). *Queer man on campus: A history of non-heterosexual college men, 1945–2000.* New York: RoutledgeFalmer.

Dolby, N. (2000). Changing selves: Multicultural education and the challenge of new identities. *Teachers College Record, 102*(5), 898–912.

D'souza, D. (1996). *The end of racism: Principles for a multiracial society.* New York: Free Press.

Duberley, J., & Johnson, P. (2011). Critical management methodology. In M. Alvesson, T. Bridgman, & H. Willmott (Eds.), *The Oxford handbook of critical management studies* (pp. 345–368). Oxford: Oxford University Press.

Eden Rock Media (Producer), & Craig, E. (Director). (2011). *Tucker & Dale vs. evil* [Motion picture]. Canada: Magnet Releasing, Reliance Big Pictures.

Edwards, K. (2006). Aspiring social justice ally identity development: A conceptual model. *NASPA Journal, 43*(4), 39–60.

Epple, D., Romano, R., & Sieg, H. (2008). Diversity and affirmative action in higher education. *Journal of Public Economic Theory, 10*(4), 475–501.

Fabiano, P., Perkins, H. W., Berkowitz, A., Linkenbach, J., & Stark, C. (2003). Engaging men as social justice allies in ending violence against women: Evidence for a social norms approach. *Journal of American College Health, 52* (3), 105–111.

Fanon, F. (2008). *Black skin, white masks* (Richard Philcox, Trans.). New York: Grove. (Original work published in 1952).

Faulkner, L. R. (2005). Address on the state of the university, September 14, 2005. Retrieved from http://www.texastop10.princeton.edu/publicity/general/UTFaulkerSpeech.pdf

Ferdman, B. M., & Gallegos, P. I. (2001). Racial identity development and Latinos in the United States. In C. L. Wijeyesinghe & B. W. Jackson III (Eds.), *New perspectives on racial identity development: A theoretical and practical anthology* (pp. 32–66). New York: New York University Press.

Fisher v. University of Texas, 631 F.3d 213 (5th Cir. 2011).

Foley, N. (2005). Becoming Hispanic: Mexican Americans and whiteness. In P. S. Rothenberg (Ed.), *White privilege. Essential readings on the other side of racism* (pp. 55–65). New York: Worth.

Forest, J. F., & Kinser, K. (2002). *Higher education in the United States: An encyclopedia.* Santa Barbara, CA: ABC-CLIO.

Forester, J. (1999). Critical ethnography: On fieldwork in a Habermasian way. In M. Alvesson & H. Willmott (Eds.), *Critical management studies* (pp. 46–65). London: Sage.

Foucault, M. (1980). Power/knowledge. In C. Gordon (Ed.), *Selected interviews and other writings, 1972–1977.* New York: Pantheon.

Freire, P. (1970). *Pedagogy of the oppressed.* New York: Herder & Herder.

Freire, P. (1985). *The politics of education: Culture, power, and liberation.* Westport, CT: Bergin & Garvey.

Freire, P. (2000). *Pedagogy of freedom: Ethics, democracy, and civic courage.* Lanham, MD: Rowman & Littlefield.

Fry, T. (2004). The struggle against "separate but equal": Teaching about Brown v. Topeka. *Southern Social Studies Journal, 30*(1), 1–30. Retrieved from www.washburn.edu/faculty/tfry/Brown%20APA%20style.pdf

Gall, J., Gall, M. D., & Borg, W. (1999). *Applying educational research: A practical guide.* New York: Addison Wesley Longman.

Garrison, J. (2010). Compassionate, spiritual, and creative listening in teaching and learning. *Teachers College Record, 112*(11), 2763–2776.

Gibson, M., & Meem, D. T. (2005). Introduction. *Journal of Lesbian Studies*, 9(4), 1–12.

Giroux, H. (1983). *Theory and resistance in education: Towards a pedagogy for the opposition*. New York: Bergin & Garvey.

Giroux, H. (2001). *Theory and resistance in education: Towards a pedagogy for the opposition, Revised and Expanded Edition*. Westport, CT: Bergin & Garvey.

Giroux, H. (2009). Critical theory and educational practice. In A. Darder, M. P. Baltodano, & R. D. Torres (Eds.), *The critical pedagogy reader* (pp. 27–51). New York: Routledge.

Goff, P., Steele, C., & Davies, P. (2008). The space between us: Stereotype threat and distance in interracial contexts. *Journal of Personality and Social Psychology, 94,* 91–107.

Goodman, D. (2000). Motivating people from privileged groups to support social justice. *Teachers College Record, 102,* 1061–1085.

Gramsci, A. (2000). *The Antonio Gramsci reader: Selected writings, 1916–1935*. E. Forgacs (Ed.). London: Lawrence & Wishart.

Gratz v. Bollinger, 539 U.S. 244 (2003).

Greenfield, T., & Ribbins, P. (Eds.). (1993). *Greenfield on educational administration: Towards a humane science*. New York: Routledge.

Grutter v. Bollinger, 539 U.S. 306 (2003).

Gurin, P., Dey, E., Hurtado, S., & Gurin, G. (2002). Diversity and higher education: Theory and impact on educational outcomes. *Harvard Educational Review, 72*(3), 330–366.

Gurin, P., Nagada, B. A., & Lopez, G. E. (2004). The benefits of diversity in education for democratic citizenship. *The Journal of Social Issues, 60*(1), 17–34.

Gutsell, J. N., & Inzlicht, M. (2010). Empathy constrained: Prejudice predicts reduced mental simulation of actions during observation of outgroups. *Journal of Experimental Social Psychology, 46,* 841–845.

Habermas, J. (1973). *Theory and practice*. Boston: Beacon Press.

Hacker, A., & Dreifus, C. (2010). *Higher education? How colleges are wasting our money and failing our kids—and what we can do about it*. New York: Macmillan.

Halperin, E. C. (2001). The Jewish problem in U.S. medical education: 1920–1955. *Journal of the History of Medicine and Allied Sciences, 56*(2), 140–167.

Handler, M. S. (1992). Introduction. In M. X (Author) & A. Haley (Collaborator), *The autobiography of Malcolm X* (pp. vii-xii). New York: Ballantine Books.

Haney Lopez, I. (1997). *White by law*. New York: New York University Press.

Harbour, W. S., & Madaus, J. W. (Eds.). (2011). *Disability services and campus dynamics*. New Directions for Higher Education, No. 154. San Francisco: Jossey-Bass.

Hardiman, R., & Jackson, B. W. (2007). Conceptual foundations for social justice courses. In M. Adams, L. A. Bell, & P. Griffin (Eds.), *Teaching for diversity and social justice: A sourcebook* (pp. 35–66). New York: Routledge.

Harper, S. R. (2008, March). *Student affairs educators as culprits in the cyclical reproduction of racism in America*. Paper presented at the meeting of the National Association of Student Personnel Administrators, Boston.

Harper, S. R. (2009). Niggers no more: A critical race counternarrative on black male student achievement at predominantly white colleges and universities. *International Journal of Qualitative Studies in Education, 22*(6), 697–712.

Harper, S. R., & Davis III, C.H.F. (2012). They (don't) care about education: A counternarrative on black male students' responses to inequitable schooling. *Educational Foundations, 26*(1), 103–120.

Harris, C. (1993). Whiteness as property. *Harvard Law Review, 106*(8), 1710–1791.

Hart, M. (2002, October 25). "South Park," in the tradition of Chaucer and Shakespeare. *The Chronicle of Higher Education*, p. B5.

Heldke, L., & O'Connor, P. (Eds.). (2004). *Oppression, privilege, & resistance: Theoretical perspectives on racism, sexism, and heterosexism.* New York: McGraw-Hill.

Helms, J. E. (1990). *Black and white racial identity theory, research, and practice.* Westport, CT: Praeger.

Herbold, H. (1994–1995). Never a level playing field: Blacks and the GI bill. *Journal of Blacks in Higher Education, 6,* 104–108.

Herman, E. S., & Chomsky, N. (1998). *Manufacturing consent: The political economy of the mass media.* New York: Vintage Books.

Heron, J. (1982). *Education of the affect.* University of London: British Postgraduate Medical Federation.

Hersh, R., & Merrow, J. (2006). *Declining by degrees: Higher education at risk.* New York: Macmillan.

hooks, b. (1994). *Teaching to transgress.* New York: Routledge.

hooks, b. (2004). Men: Comrades in struggle. In M. S. Kimmel & M. A. Messner (Eds.), *Men's lives* (pp. 68–83). Needham Heights, MA: Allyn & Bacon.

Hopwood v. Texas, 78 F.3d 932 (5th Cir. 1996), cert. denied, 518 U.S. 1033 (1996).

Horkheimer, M. (1974). *Eclipse of reason.* New York: Seabury Press.

Horn, C., & Flores, S. (2003). *Percent plans in college admissions: A comparative analysis of three states' experiences.* Cambridge, MA: The Civil Rights Project at Harvard University.

Horowitz, H. L. (1987). *Campus life: Undergraduate cultures from the end of the eighteenth century to the present.* Chicago: University of Chicago Press.

Horse, P. G. (2001). Reflections on American Indian identity. In C. L. Wijeyesinghe & B. W. Jackson III (Eds.), *New perspectives on racial identity development: A theoretical and practical anthology* (pp. 91–107). New York: New York University Press.

Howe, N., & Strauss, W. (2000). *Millennials rising: The next great generation.* New York: Vintage Books.

H. R. Rep. No. 94–332, at 5 (1975).

Hu, S., & Kuh, G. D. (2003). Diversity experiences and college student learning and personal development. *Journal of College Student Development, 44*(3), 320–334.

Hurtado, S. (2001). Linking diversity and educational purpose: How diversity affects the classroom environment and student development. In G. Orfield (Ed.), *Diversity challenged: Evidence on the impact of affirmative action* (pp. 187–203). Cambridge, MA: Harvard Educational.

Huston, T. (2009). *Teaching what you don't know.* Cambridge, MA: Harvard University Press.

Jackson, J. (2008). *Racial paranoia: The unintended consequences of political correctness.* New York: Perseus Books.

Jayakumar, U. M. (2008). Can higher education meet the needs of an increasingly diverse and global society? Campus diversity and cross-cultural workforce competencies. *Harvard Educational Review, 78*(4), 615–651.

Jensen, R. (2004). *Writing dissent: Taking radical ideas from the margins to the mainstream.* New York: Peter Lang.

Jingo, M. (Producer), & Kurosawa, A. (Director). (1950). *Rashomon* [Motion picture]. Japan: Daiei Film Co., Ltd. United States: RKO Radio Pictures.

Johnson, A. (2006). *Power, privilege, and difference.* New York: McGraw-Hill.

Johnson v. Board of Regents of the University of Georgia, 263 F.3d 1234 (11th. Cir. 2001).

Jones, K. (1988). Buddhism and social action. In F. Eppsteiner (Ed.), *The path of compassion: Writings on socially engaged Buddhism* (pp. 65–81). Berkeley, CA: Parallax Press.

Jones, S. R., & McEwen, M. K. (2000). A conceptual model of multiple dimensions of identity. *Journal of College Student Development, 41,* 405–414.

Josselson, R. (1996). *Revising herself: The story of women's identity from college to midlife.* New York: Oxford University Press.

Kahlenberg, R. D. (2012a). *A better affirmative action: State universities that created alternatives to racial preferences.* Century Foundation Report. New York: Century Foundation Press.

Kahlenberg, R. D. (2012b, July 2). Magnifying social inequality. *The Chronicle of Higher Education.* Retrieved from http://chronicle.com/article/Magnifying -Social-Inequality/132627

Kahneman, D. (2011). *Thinking fast and slow.* New York: Farrar, Straus, and Giroux.

Kane, T. J. (1998). Misconceptions in the debate over affirmative action in college admissions. In G. Orfield & E. Miller (Eds.), *Chilling admissions: The affirmative action crisis and the search for alternatives* (pp. 17–30). Cambridge: Harvard Education.

Karabel, J. (1998). No alternative: The effect of color-blind in California. In G. Orfield & E. Miller (Eds.), *Chilling admissions. The affirmative action crisis and the search for alternatives* (pp. 33–49). Cambridge, MA: Harvard Education.

Katz, D., & Kahn, R. (2005). Organizations and the systems concept. In J. Shafritz, J. Ott, & Y. Jang (Eds.), *Classics of organization theory* (pp. 480–490). Belmont, CA: Thomson Wadsworth.

Katznelson, I. (2005). *When affirmative action was white: An untold history of racial inequality in twentieth-century America.* New York: Norton.

Kaufman, M. (1999). Men, feminism, and men's contradictory experiences of power. In J. A. Kuypers (Ed.), *Men and power.* Halifax, Nova Scotia: Fernwood Books.

Kegan, R. (1982). *The evolving self: Problem and process in human development.* Cambridge, MA: Harvard University Press.

Kegan, R. (1994). *In over our heads: The mental demands of modern life.* Cambridge, MA: Harvard University Press.

Kegan, R., & Lahey, L. (2009). *Immunity to change: How to overcome it and unlock the potential in yourself and your organization.* Boston: Harvard Business Review Press.

Kelly, C. (2008). White men: An exploration of intersections of masculinity, whiteness and colonialism and the engagement of counter-hegemonic projects. In E. Uchendu (Ed.), *Masculinities in contemporary Africa* (pp. 110–132). Council for the Development of Social Science Research in Africa, Dakar, Senegal: Imprimerie Saint-Paul.

Kendall, F. (2006). *Understanding white privilege: Creating pathways to authentic relationships across race.* New York: Routledge.

Kieffer, C. (1981, April). *Doing "dialogic retrospection": Approaching empowerment through participatory research.* Paper presented at the International Meeting of the Society for Applied Anthropology, Edinburgh, Scotland.

Kim, J. (2001). Asian American identity development theory. In C. L. Wijeyesinghe & B. W. Jackson III (Eds.), *New perspectives on racial identity development: A theoretical and practical anthology* (pp. 67–90). New York: New York University Press.

Kincheloe, J. L. (2005). *Critical constructivism primer.* New York: Peter Lang.

Kinsler, K. (2010). The utility of educational action research for emancipatory change. *Action Research* 8(2), 171–189.

Kirp, D. (2003). *Shakespeare, Einstein, and the bottom line: The marketing of higher education.* Cambridge, MA: Harvard University Press.

Kivel, P. (2002). *Uprooting racism: How white people can work for racial justice.* Gabriola Island, B.C., Canada: New Society Publishers.

Knights, D. (2011). Power at work in organizations. In M. Alvesson, T. Bridgeman, & H. Willmont (Eds.), *The Oxford handbook of critical management studies* (pp. 144–165). New York: Oxford University Press.

Kolling, A. T. (1998). Student affirmative action and the courts. In D. D. Gehring (Ed.), *Responding to the new affirmative action climate* (pp. 15–31). San Francisco: Jossey-Bass.

Kronman, A. (2007). *Education's end: Why our colleges and universities have given up on the meaning of life.* New Haven, CT: Yale University Press.

Kuklinski, J. H. (2006). The scientific study of campus diversity and students' educational outcomes. *Public Opinion Quarterly, 70*(1), 99–120.

Lagemann, E. C. (2012). *What is college for? The public purpose of higher education.* New York: Teachers College Press.

Laker, J. (2003). Bad dogs: Rethinking our engagement of male students. In P. Brown (Ed.), *Men: On campus.* Washington, DC: Standing Committee for Men, American College Personnel Association.

Lee, E. (1999). *Academic excellence and anti-racism.* Cambridge, MA: Centre for Anti-Racist Education.

Levstik, L. S., & Barton, K. C. (2010). *Doing history: Investigating with children in elementary and middle schools.* New York: Routledge.

Linne, R. (2007). Queer youths reframing media culture. In D. Macedo & S. Steinberg (Eds.), *Media literacy: A reader* (pp. 463–470). New York: Peter Lang.

Litolff, E. H. (2007). Higher education desegregation: An analysis of state efforts in systems formerly operating segregated systems of higher education. Retrieved from Louisiana State University Electronic Thesis and Dissertation Collection (No. etd-06072007–073810).

Loes, C. N., Pascarella, E. T., & Umbach, P. D. (2012). Effects of diversity experiences on critical thinking skills: Who benefits? *Journal of Higher Education, 83*(1), 1–25.

Loewen, J. W. (1995). *Lies my teacher told me: Everything your American history textbook got wrong.* New York: Simon & Schuster.

Loewen, J. W. (1999). *Lies across America: What our historic sites get wrong.* New York: Simon & Schuster.

Long, M. (2004). College applications and the effect of affirmative action. *Journal of Econometrics, 121*(1–2), 319–342.

Marcia, J. (2002). Identity and psychosocial development in adulthood. *Identity: An International Journal of Theory and Research, 2*(1), 7–28.

Marcuse, H. (1960). *Reason and revolution.* Boston: Beacon Press.

Margo, R. (1990). The impact of separate-but-equal. In R. Margo (Ed.), *Race and schooling in the south, 1880–1950: An economic history* (pp. 68–86). Chicago: University of Chicago Press. Retrieved from http://www.nber.org/chapters/c8795

Markus, H., & Moya, P. (2010). *Doing race: 21 essays for the 21st century.* New York: Norton.

Mason, M., Wolfinger, N., & Goulden, M. (2013). *Do babies matter? Gender and family in the ivory tower.* New Brunswick, NJ: Rutgers University Press.

McCall, L. (2005). The complexity of intersectionality. *Signs, 30,* 1771–1800.

McIntosh, P. (1988). *White privilege and male privilege: A personal account of coming to see correspondences through work in women's studies.* Wellesley, MA: Wellesley College Center for Research on Women.

McLaren, P. (2009). Critical pedagogy: A look at the major concepts. In A. Darder, M. P. Baltodano, & R. D. Torres (Eds.), *The critical pedagogy reader* (pp. 61–83). New York: Routledge.

McWhorter, J. (2008, December 30). Racism in America is over. *Forbes.* Retrieved from http://www.forbes.com/2008/12/30/end-of-racism-oped-cx_jm_1230mcwhorter.html

Meier, D. (2002). *The power of their ideas: Lessons for America from a small school in Harlem.* Boston: Beacon Press.

Mertens, D., Sullivan, M., & Stace, H. (2011). Disability communities: Transformative research for social justice. In N. K. Denzin & Y. S. Lincoln (Eds.), *Handbook of qualitative research.* Thousand Oaks, CA: Sage.

Meyerson, D. (2001). *Tempered radicals: How people use difference to inspire change at work.* Boston: Harvard Business School Press.

Milem, J. (2003). The educational benefits of diversity: Evidence from multiple sectors. In M. J. Chang, D. Witt, J. Jones, & K. Hakuta (Eds.), *Compelling interest: Examining the evidence on racial dynamics in colleges and universities.* (pp. 126–169). Palo Alto, CA: Stanford University Press.

Milgram, S. (1974). *Obedience to authority: An experimental view.* New York: HarperCollins.

Mill, J. S. (1859). On liberty. *Library of Economics and Liberty.* Retrieved from http://www.econlib.org/library/Mill/mlLbty.html

Miller, T. (2003). Governmentality or commodification? U.S. higher education. *Cultural Studies, 19*(6), 897–904.

Moore, S., & Kuol, N. (2007). Matters of the heart: Exploring the emotional dimensions of educational experience in recollected accounts of excellent teaching. *International Journal for Academic Development, 12*(2), 87–98.

Moreno, P. B. (2003). The history of affirmative action law and its relation to college admission. *Journal of College Admission, 179,* 14–21.

Morgan, G. (2006). *Images of organization.* London: Sage.

Morgan, G., & Spicer, A. (2011). Critical approaches to organizational change. In M. Alvesson, T. Bridgman, & H. Willmott (Eds.), *The Oxford handbook of critical management studies* (pp. 213–231). Oxford: Oxford University Press.

Mortiboys, A. (2012). *Teaching with emotional intelligence: A step-by-step guide for higher and further education professionals.* New York: Routledge.

Moses, M., Yun, J., & Marin, P. (2009). Affirmative action's fate: Are 20 more years enough? *Education Policy Analysis Archives, 17*(17). Retrieved from http://epaa.asu.edu/epaa/v17n17

Mundell, C. (2011). Far from perfection, closer than ever before: Employing new forums to facilitate dialogues about race. In P. Magolda & M. Baxter Magolda (Eds.), *Contested issues in student affairs: Diverse perspectives and respectful dialogues* (pp. 236–243). Sterling, VA: Stylus.

Murray, A. (2006). *Paradigm found: Leading and managing for positive change.* Novato, CA: New World Library.

Musen, K. (Producer & Director), & Zimbardo, P. G. (Writer). (1992). *Quiet rage: The Stanford prison study* [Documentary film]. New York: Insight Media.

Nash, R. (2001). One group, many truths: Constructing a moral conversation. In R. Nash (Ed.), *Religious pluralism in the academy: Opening the dialogue* (pp. 165–206). New York: Peter Lang.

National Center for Education Statistics. (2005). *2003–04 National postsecondary student aid study* (NPSAS: 04). Washington, DC: U.S. Department of Education.

National Center for Education Statistics. (2012). *Digest of education statistics, 2011* (NCES 2012–001). Washington, DC: U.S. Department of Education.

Nord, W., & Jermier, J. (1999). Critical social science for managers? Promising and perverse possibilities. In M. Alvesson & H. Willmont (Eds.), *Critical management studies* (pp. 202–222). Newbury Park, CA: Sage.

Nussbaum, M. (2010). *Not for profit: Why democracy needs the humanities.* Princeton, NJ: Princeton University Press.

Okin, S. (1999). *Is multiculturalism bad for women?* Princeton, NJ: Princeton University Press.

Ollhoff, J., & Walcheski, M. (2002). *Stepping into wholes: Introduction to complex systems.* Eden Prairie, MN: Sparrow Media Group.

Onkst, D. H. (1998). First a Negro ... incidentally a veteran: Black World War Two veterans and the G.I. bill of rights in the Deep South, 1944–1948. *Journal of Social History, 31*(3), 517–543.

Palmer, P. J. (2004). *A hidden wholeness: The journey toward an undivided life.* San Francisco: Jossey-Bass.

Palmer, P. J. (2007). *The courage to teach: Exploring the inner landscape of a teacher's life* (10th anniv. ed.). San Francisco: Jossey-Bass.

Park, J. (2011). The elephant in the room—Race. In P. Magolda & M. Baxter Magolda (Eds.), *Contested issues in student affairs: Diverse perspectives and respectful dialogues* (pp. 225–235). Sterling, VA: Stylus.

Parks, S. D. (2005). *Leadership can be taught: A bold approach for a complex world.* Boston: Harvard Business School.

Parnell, C. S. (2008). Christian persecution in public schools. *Free Republic*, 1–4. Retrieved from http://www.freerepublic.com/focus/f-bloggers/1954210/posts

Pascarella, E., & Terenzini, P. (2005). *How college affects students: A third decade of research.* San Francisco: Jossey-Bass.

Patton, L. D., Shahjahan, R., & Osei-Kofi, N. (2010). Emergent approaches to diversity and social justice in higher education. *Equity and Excellence in Education, 43*(3), 265–278.

Paul, R., & Elder, L. (2006). *Critical thinking: Tools for taking charge of your learning and your life.* Upper Saddle River, NJ: Prentice Hall.

Peltier Campbell, K. (2012). Making excellence inclusive: Higher education's LGBTQ contexts. *Diversity & Democracy, 15*(1), 1.

Perrucci, R., & Wyson, E. (2002). *The new class society.* Lanham, MD: Rowman & Littlefield.

Perry, W. G. (1970). *Forms of intellectual and ethical development in the college years: A scheme.* Troy, MO: Holt, Rinehart, & Winston.

Phinney, J. S. (1993). A three-stage model of ethnic identity development in adolescence. In M. E. Bernal & G. P. Knight (Eds.), *Ethnic identity formation and transmission among Hispanic and other minorities* (pp. 61–79). Albany: State University of New York Press.

Piaget, J. (1954). *The construction of reality in the child* (M. Cook, Trans.). New York: Basic Books.

Rankin, S., Blumenfeld, W. J., Weber, G. N., & Frazer, S. (2010). *State of higher education for LGBT people: Campus Pride 2010 National College Climate Survey.* Charlotte, NC: Campus Pride.

Rasmussen, S. (2012). 55% Oppose affirmative action policies for college admissions. Retrieved from http://www.rasmussenreports.com/public_content /politics/general_politics/february_2012/55_oppose_affirmative_action_policies _for_college_admissions

Reardon, S. F. (2011). The widening academic achievement gap between the rich and the poor: New evidence and possible explanations. In G. J. Duncan & R. Murnane (Eds.), *Whither opportunity: Rising inequality, schools, and children's life chances* (pp. 91–116). New York: Russell Sage Foundation.

Reason, R., Broido, E., Davis, T., & Evans, N. (2005). *Developing social justice allies.* New Directions in Student Services, No. 110. San Francisco: Jossey-Bass.

Regents of the University of California v. Bakke, 438 U.S. 265 (1978).

Rogers, C. (1961). *On becoming a person: A therapist's view of psychotherapy.* New York: Houghton Mifflin.

Said, E. (2001). In the shadow of the West. In G. Viswanathan (Ed.), *Power, politics and culture: Interviews with Edward W. Said* (pp. 39–52). New York: Vintage Books.

Said, E. (2002). *Power, politics, and culture.* New York: Pantheon Books.

Scharmer, O. C. (2007). *Theory u: Leading from the future as it emerges.* Cambridge, MA: Society for Organizational Learning.

Schuford, B. C. (1998). Recommendations for the future. In D. D. Gehring (Ed.), *Responding to the new affirmative action climate* (pp. 71–78). New Directions for Student Services, No. 125. San Francisco: Jossey-Bass.

Senge, P. M. (1994). *The fifth discipline: The art and practice of the learning organization*. New York: Doubleday.

Senge, P. M., Scharmer, C. O., Jaworski, J., & Flowers, B. (2008). *Presence: Human purpose and the field of the future*. New York: Doubleday.

Shafritz, J. Ott, J., & Jang, Y. (2005). *Classics of organization theory*. Belmont, CA: Thomson Wadsworth.

Shields, S. (2008). Gender: An intersectionality perspective. *Sex Roles, 59*, 301–311.

Silver, J. (Producer), & Wachowski, A., & Wachowski, L. (Directors). (1999). *The matrix* [Motion picture]. United States: Warner Bros.

Silverblatt, A, Ferry, J., & Finan, B. (1999). *Approaches to media literacy: A handbook*. London: M.E. Sharpe.

Sinn, M. (2012, September 3). Government spends more on corporate welfare subsidies than social welfare programs. Retrieved from http://thinkby numbers.org/government-spending/corporate-welfare/corporate-welfare -statistics-vs-social-welfare-statistics

Sleeter, C., & Grant, C. (1994). *Making choices for multicultural education: Five approaches to race, class, and gender*. New York: Merrill.

Smith, L., Bratini, L., Chambers, D., Jensen, R. V., & Romero, L. (2010). Between idealism and reality: Meeting the challenges of participatory action research. *Action Research, 8*(407), 407–425.

Smith, Z. (2010, December). Generation why? *New York Review of Books*. Retrieved from http://www.nybooks.com/articles/archives/2010/nov/25 /generation-why/?pagination=false

Solomon, B. (1985). *In the company of educated women*. New Haven, CT: Yale University Press.

Spalding, M. (2010, October 1). Why is America exceptional? Retrieved from http://www.heritage.org/research/reports/2010/09/why-is-america-exceptional

Stone, D., Patton, B., & Heen, S. (2000). *Difficult conversations: How to discuss what matters most.* New York: Penguin.

Stone, J. (2007). *When she was white: The true story of a family divided by race.* New York: Miramax Books.

Sue, D. W. (2010). *Microaggressions in everyday life: Race, gender, and sexual orientation.* Hoboken, NJ: Wiley.

Swain, M. H., Payne, E. A., & Spruill, M. J. (Eds.). (2010). *Mississippi women: Their histories, their lives.* Athens: University of Georgia Press.

Takacs, D. (2002). Positionality, epistemology, and social justice in the classroom. *Social Justice, 29*(4) 168–181.

Takaki, R. (1993). *A different mirror: A history of multicultural America.* Boston: Little, Brown.

Takaki, R. (1998). *Strangers from a different shore: The history of Asian Americans.* Boston: Little, Brown.

Tatum, B. (1997). *"Why are all the black kids sitting together in the cafeteria?" and other conversations about race.* New York: Basic Books.

Taylor, M. (2010). *Crisis on campus: A bold plan for reforming our colleges and universities.* New York: Random House.

Tornblom, K. Y., & Vermunt, R. (2007). Towards an integration of distributive justice, procedural justice, and social resource theories. *Social Justice Research, 20*(3), 312–335.

Torres, V., Jones, S. R., & Renn. K. A. (2009). Identity development theories in student affairs: Origins, current status, and new approaches. *Journal of College Student Development, 50*(6), 577–596.

Tuchman, G. (1978). *Making news: A study in the construction of reality.* New York: Macmillan.

Tuchman, G. (2009). *Wannabe U: Inside the corporate university.* Chicago: University of Chicago Press.

Tuitt, F., Hanna, M., Martinez, L., Salazar, M., & Griffin, R. (2009). Teaching in the line of fire: Faculty of color in the academy. *The NEA Higher Education Journal*, Fall, 65–74.

Turner, C., Gonzalez, J., & Wood, J. L. (2008). Faculty of color in academe: What 20 years of literature tells us. *Journal of Diversity in Higher Education*, 1(3), 139–168.

Turner, S., & Bound, J. (2003). Closing the gap or widening the divide: The effects of the G.I. bill and World War II on the educational outcomes of black Americans. *Journal of Economic History*, 63(1), 145–177.

Twenge, J. M. (2006). *Generation me: Why today's young Americans are more confident, assertive, entitled—and more miserable than ever before*. New York: Free Press.

Tyson, L. (2006). *Critical theory today: A user-friendly guide*. New York: Routledge.

United States v. Bhagat Singh Thind, 261 U.S. 204 (1923).

U.S. Department of Justice. (2012). *Equal access to education: Forty years of Title IX*. Washington, DC: Author.

Vercic, D., & Grunig, J. (2000). The origins of public relations theory in economics and strategic management. In D. Moss, D. Vercic, & G. Warnaby (Eds.), *Perspectives on public relations research* (pp. 9–48). New York: Routledge.

Voronov, M., & Coleman, P. (2003). Beyond the ivory towers: Organizational power practices and a "practical" critical postmodernism. *Journal of Applied Behavioral Science*, 39(169), 169–185.

Vygotsky, L. S. (1978). *Mind in society: The development of higher psychological processes* (M. Cook, Trans.). Cambridge, MA: Harvard University Press.

Wall, V. A., & Evans, N. J. (Eds.). (1999). *Toward acceptance: Sexual orientation issues on campus*. Lanham, MD: University Press of America.

Washburn, J. (2005). *University inc.: The corporate corruption of higher education*. New York: Basic Books.

Wasley, P. (2006). Accreditor of education schools drops controversial "social justice" language. *Chronicle of Higher Education, 52*(41), A13.

Weber, L. (1998). A conceptual framework for understanding race, class, gender, and sexuality. *Psychology of Women Quarterly, 22,* 13–32.

Weigert, K. M., & Crews, R. J. (Eds.). (1999). *Teaching for justice: Concepts and models for service-learning in peace studies*. Reston, VA: American Association for Higher Education.

Weiler, K. (2009). Feminist analysis of gender and schooling. In A. Darder, M. P. Baltodano, & R. D. Torres (Eds.), *The critical pedagogy reader* (pp. 217–239). New York: Routledge.

Wheatley, M. (2006). *Leadership and the new science: Discovering order in a chaotic world*. San Francisco: Berrett-Koehler.

Wijeyesinghe, C. L. (2001). Racial identity in multiracial people: An alternative paradigm. In C. L. Wijeyesinghe & B. W. Jackson III (Eds.), *New perspectives on racial identity development: A theoretical and practical anthology* (pp. 129–152). New York: New York University Press.

Wineburg, S. (2001). *Historical thinking and other unnatural acts: Charting the future of teaching the past*. Philadelphia: Temple University Press.

Wintonick, M. (Producer) & Achbar, M. (Director). (1992). *Manufacturing consent: Noam Chomsky and the media* [Motion picture]. Canada: Zeitgeist Films.

Wolff, E. N. (2010). *Recent trends in household wealth in the United States: Rising debt and the middle-class squeeze—an update to 2007* (Working Paper No. 589). Annandale-on-Hudson, NY: The Levy Economics Institute of Bard College.

Yamato, G. (2004). Something about the subject makes it hard to name. In L. Heldke & P. O'Connor (Eds.), *Oppression, privilege, and resistance: Theoretical perspectives on racism, sexism, and heterosexism* (pp. 64–75). New York: McGraw-Hill.

Young, I. (2004). Five faces of oppression. In L. Heldke & P. O'Connor (Eds.), *Oppression, privilege, & resistance: Theoretical perspectives on racism, sexism, and heterosexism* (pp. 37–63). New York: McGraw Hill.

Zemsky, R., Wegner, G., & Massy, W. (2006). *Remaking the American university: Market-smart and mission-centered.* New Brunswick, NJ: Rutgers University Press.

Zimbardo, P. (2007). *The Lucifer effect: Understanding how good people turn evil.* New York: Random House.

Zine, J. (2001). Negotiating equity: The dynamics of minority community engagement in constructing inclusive education policy. *The Cambridge Journal of Education, 31*(2), 239–269.

Zinn, H. (1968). *Disobedience and democracy: Nine fallacies on law and order.* Cambridge, MA: South End Press.

Zinn, H. (1990). *The politics of history.* Champaign: University of Illinois Press.

Zinn, H. (2004, September 20). The optimism of uncertainty. *The Nation.* Retrieved from http://www.thenation.com/article/optimism-uncertainty

Zinn, H. (2005). *A people's history of the United States: 1492–present.* New York: Harper Perennial Modern Classics.

Name Index

e represents exhibit; *t* represents table.

Subject Index